They All
Fall Down
To Worship

They All Fall Down

To Worship

Six Women, One Family,
Changed Forever

BARB PAGEL AND
LORI MCCONCHIE

TATE PUBLISHING & Enterprises

Published by Tate Publishing & Enterprises, LLC
127 E. Trade Center Terrace | Mustang, Oklahoma 73064 USA
1.888.361.9473 | www.tatepublishing.com

Tate Publishing is committed to excellence in the publishing industry. The company reflects the philosophy established by the founders, based on Psalm 68:11,
"The Lord gave the word and great was the company of those who published it."

Book design copyright © 2011 by Tate Publishing, LLC. All rights reserved.
Cover design by Lauran Levy
Interior design by Lindsay B. Behrens

Published in the United States of America

ISBN: 978-1-61739-915-2
1. Religion / Christian Life / Women's Issues
2. Religion / Christian Life / Inspirational
11.02.24

We want to dedicate this book to our Lord and Savior, Jesus Christ, for in Him, we live and move and exist (Acts 17:28, NLT).

Table of Contents

Introduction:
Note from Lori

I once heard someone say, "There are three kinds of people in this world: believers, unbelievers, and make-believers." My sisters and I were in the last two categories. One of us had never even heard about God, and the rest of us said we believed in God, but our lives showed just the opposite: "Such people claim they know God, but they deny Him by the way they live" (Titus 1:16, NIV).

Most of the time we fooled the people around us, but what was worse, we had fooled ourselves. We were all talk without a walk, and there was no evidence of a saving faith in our lives. The faith that we claimed to have was born out of a religion and not a relationship with Jesus. This kind of faith couldn't save us. Why? Because it wasn't from God. A faith that does not cause a person to turn from sin and self to God is no faith at all.

Salvation is supernatural. It is a miraculous transformation of the soul that gives us the desire and power to obey Him. "For God is working in you, giving you the desire and the power to do what pleases Him" (Philippians 2:13, NLT). It is a new life, a gift from God, and it involves a complete change of heart, mind, purpose, and direction. And because of this, a person can never claim to have faith in God and not grow in their love for Him. This newfound love for God is real and lasting because it is not based on our efforts but on the saving work of God.

That's what this book is about—God's transforming grace in the lives of four sisters and two sisters-in-law. *They All Fall Down…to Worship* is a story so unbelievable that it could only have been possible through the saving work of God. You will hear from each one of us as we tell our story of how God reached down and, one by one, placed a new heart within us and caused us to be born again (1 Peter 1:3). We had no idea what God was about to do in each of our lives.

We hope this book will inspire and encourage believers, and it is our utmost prayer that it will be used by God to open the eyes of unbelievers. Last, but not least, we pray that it will deliver make-believers out of the clutches of deception and into the arms of the one and only Lord and Savior, Jesus Christ, so that together we can all fall down…to worship!

...the twenty-four elders fall down before Him who is seated on the throne and worship Him who lives forever and ever. They cast their crowns before the throne, saying, "Worthy are You, our Lord and God, to receive glory and honor and power, for You created all things, and by Your will they existed and were created."

Revelation 4:10–11 (ESV)

Lori

From Death to Life:
Lori's Story

I assure you, those who listen to My message and believe in God who sent Me have eternal life. They will never be condemned for their sins, but they have already passed from death into life.

1 John 5:24 (NLT)

*R*rring rrrring. The shrill sound of a telephone invaded my sleep. Half awake, I fumbled for the phone when my eyes caught the subtle red glow of the alarm clock. Four a.m.! *Who would be calling at this hour?* I thought. After locating the phone, I answered and was greeted by a rough voice on the other end.

"Can I speak to Bob?" he asked. Bob was already sitting up in bed when I handed him the phone. "This is the California Highway Patrol," he said. "You need to come to your mother's house immediately."

Bob could not get dressed fast enough. His mind was spinning as he grabbed his keys and raced out the door. His mom lived right around the corner, and the patrolman met him in the driveway.

"There's been an accident," he said. "It was your brother, and it was fatal."

Kirk was only twenty four years old. He was driving home on the freeway when his car, for some unknown reason, lost control and was hit by another vehicle. The driver of the vehicle did not stop. Kirk's car flipped three times and came to rest on its top. They found his body face-down on the freeway after a second vehicle struck him. The driver of the second vehicle called the police and waited until they arrived.

When I found out what happened, every emotion I ever knew came to the surface. I was devastated. I loved Kirk so much, and I could not imagine how Bob would ever get over the loss of his brother—his best friend. How was I going to help him get through this? That's when reality hit and fear gripped my heart. Life isn't forever. My mind was flooded with questions. *How could this happen? We had just seen him the night before. One minute he was here, the next he was gone. If it happened to Kirk, it could happen to anyone. Where did he go?* I will never forget the fear, anxiety, and confusion I felt at that moment. Watching Bob go through this agonizing loss over the next weeks and months was almost too much to bear. I thought I had all the answers to life, but now I had only questions.

———————

My thoughts went back to my days in high school when I began a "Dear God" diary. I had heard about God while growing up, but I had no idea who He was. I went to church on Sundays, but I never enjoyed being there. It was a duty that was dry and dull, just like my heart. I believed in God (or so I thought), and I confessed my sins and tried to be good, so I could go to heaven and not hell. But the truth was, I didn't know where I was going when I died.

I always felt like there was something missing in my life. I really didn't know what I was searching for, but whatever it was, I knew I didn't have it. Because of that, I spent all of my high school years trying to make a relationship work that I thought would fulfill my life and bring me true happiness. The thought of having my boyfriend love me outweighed my desire for anything else, so I pursued it with a passion. On and on it went. Every day was a roller coaster of doubts and insecurities. I made all of my decisions based on the way I felt at any given moment. If he liked me, I felt good; if he didn't, I felt worthless. Needless to say, all of my worth was wrapped up in the status of that relationship. That's why I started my "Dear God" diary. I needed to sort out all of my thoughts and writing them down seemed to help. I didn't know if God loved me or if He could hear me at all. I wanted to get close to Him, but He seemed far away and much too busy for someone like me. All my efforts to reach Him were futile.

Several weeks after I graduated, I went to visit my sister, Kerry. She had recently moved to California with Donna, who we didn't know at the time would become our future sister-in-law. Orange County was huge compared to my small hometown in Nebraska where everyone knew everything about everybody, not to mention it was over a thousand miles away. Once I got there, I realized it would be the perfect place to get away from the watchful eye of all my peers. I was especially relieved to get away from the high school relationship that was making me miserable.

I phoned my parents and told them I wouldn't be coming home. As I started my life in California, I lived for the moment and had only one goal—to be happy. Donna and I got jobs as waitresses and worked the graveyard shift, so we could spend every day at the beach and every night at Disneyland. That was my life: work, the beach, and the "happiest place on earth." At seventeen, I felt like life couldn't have been better. So why did I feel so empty?

The next few years, I dated off and on but quickly tired of that whole scene. Being a waitress made it difficult to stay away from the superficial advances from some of my customers. There was, however, one regular customer I enjoyed waiting on because he always made me laugh. Every time Randy came into the restaurant, he insisted that I meet a friend of his. A friend that *he said* would be *perfect* for me. Despite the fact that I repeatedly told him I was not interested, he brought him in anyway and introduced us. I reached over the table and shook Bob's hand. *There, I met him. Now maybe Randy will give up trying to be a matchmaker.*

Bob started coming in for lunch almost every day, and as much as I hated to admit it, there was something about him that was different. It was the way he made me feel when he looked at me. He seemed honest and real, almost like he cared deeply for me even though we had just met. There was no pretense about him.

Randy continued to be persistent in his efforts to get us together, and it finally paid off. Bob and I were going on our first date. His family was going to be celebrating his brother Kirk's twenty-first birthday, and his mom, aunts, uncles, and even grandparents would be there. *No pressure!* By the time the night was over, I had laughed so hard my stomach hurt. Bob really knew how to make me laugh. Not only that, but his family was amazing.

Bob and his brother, Kirk, were raised by a single mom, and they were very close. This was one of the things that attracted me to him. He cared for his younger brother as a father cares for his son. He played all the roles: protector for his mom, and father and friend to his brother. He had a deep love for them, and it made me want to know him more.

Whenever we went out together, Bob was a perfect gentleman. I loved being with him and always felt safe and protected. Before long, we were going out almost every night. I wanted to live closer to him, so I was thrilled when his aunt and uncle asked me to move into their guest house. For the first time in my life, I had met somebody who seemed to know me better than I knew myself, and it scared me. Our relationship was better than anything I had ever experienced, but things were moving fast, and I didn't know how to handle it. Bob was ready for a commitment, and I was ready to run. He loved me with his whole heart, but I couldn't help wondering if *my* heart was still with my old boyfriend from high school. Kevin and I began dating when I was a freshman and our relationship was off and on for years. I needed some time to sort out my thoughts, and the only place I could think about going was home. I needed to see him, and that's where he was.

I didn't know how I was going to tell Bob I was leaving. I was torn and at the same time convinced I couldn't move on with him unless I was ready to completely give my heart to him. When I finally told him, Bob was devastated. His heart was broken, but all he wanted was for me to be happy. I told him he would be the first to know if I wasn't coming back. Leaving him was one of the hardest things I've ever done, but it was something I knew I had to do.

The fifteen-hundred-mile drive home was anything but joyful. I couldn't erase from my mind the look on Bob's face when I said goodbye. I didn't even know *what* to think anymore. *Am I doing the right thing? Am I going home for nothing?*

I ran into my old boyfriend soon after arriving back home, and he asked me if I wanted to go out. Without hesitation, I said yes. I couldn't wait! As I was getting ready, I wondered if we would get back together and make it work this time. He picked me up, and there was a lot of small talk and just trying to catch up. As the night went on, we talked about some things from our past that ended in a disagreement. Neither of us was willing to compromise. When he dropped me off, we didn't talk about going out again. I was so heartbroken and disappointed, but I still didn't think it was over. My only thought was, *Now what?*

Two weeks later, a friend of mine from high school invited me to live with her in Lincoln, Nebraska. It was a hundred and fifty miles away. Having no other plans, and not knowing what else to do, I decided to make the move. Bob and I continued to call each other and wrote letters often.

August 23, 1976
Lori,

It's amazing all the things that remind me of you. It's only been two weeks, but it seems like two years. Each day gets a little easier, but it's tough…Before you left, I could have talked to you around the clock, and now I can't even fill up a page.

Love, Bob xxxooo

I searched everywhere for a job when I got to Lincoln, but no one would hire me. I called my mom almost every day crying, and I was getting more desperate as time went on. I had no money, and my bills were piling up. I had applied at an upscale restaurant, but the only opening they had was in the bar as a cocktail waitress. I turned them down because I did not want to work in that environment, *let alone in those uniforms,* but after weeks of looking, and no job in sight, I reluctantly called and told them I would take it. This was the last place on earth I wanted to be.

I became friends with a girl at work. She was the bartender and knew a lot of people. We would go to the bars every night after our shift and stay until they closed. I had occasionally smoked pot before, but now smoking pot and drinking became the norm for our nights out. I had turned into the kind of person I never wanted to be. I was depressed and felt empty and alone, and my relationship with Bob was slowly deteriorating.

September 17, 1976
You know, Lori, for the first time in my life I realize there is someone who really gives me strength. The only problem is she's a million miles away from me…

October 8, 1976
I hope you still think about me sometimes. I think about you all the time because I love you more than you will ever know.
    Bob

November 20, 1976
Lori, I really do care about you, and if things never turn out between you and me, I still care if you are happy or not. So be happy, okay? You know things really changed in my life after I met you. I've already told you, but those four months were the best…

December 20, 1976
You know you won't believe this, but I just can't think of anything to say. All the things we used to talk about don't seem important anymore. I really wish I could think of things to tell you that would matter to you. I hope we never get too far apart. I miss you, Lori…

It had been four months since I had moved to Lincoln. It was Christmas, and I couldn't wait to go home. I went over to my brother's house to see him. Dave had always been friends with my old boyfriend, but I had no idea Kevin would show up at his house that day. He walked in and sat down beside me and told me that he had been thinking a lot lately. He asked me if I would give him another chance, and said he would do whatever it took to make our relationship work. He said he didn't want to lose me forever, and that he wanted to spend the rest of his life with me. He had never said those words before. *Maybe we could put everything behind us and start over. After all, this is what I had come back for...wasn't it?*

One of the first things I knew I had to do was write to Bob. I told him that I had gotten back with Kevin, and I wouldn't be coming back. Bob told me later he felt both sad and relieved after reading my letter. He threw it away, and I never heard from him again. That was the only letter of mine he didn't keep.

In the few months that followed, things between Kevin and I were better than they had ever been. But no matter how well things were going, or how much fun we had together, I silently questioned if this was all there was. I had chased this dream for years, and now that I had it, why wasn't I satisfied? He seemed to be perfectly content with the way things were going, and I should have been too, so what was missing? Maybe

I was trying to make something work that was never there. Maybe this had just been a high school relationship and nothing more.

As time went on, I could not escape the endless thoughts and questions I had. The more I was with Kevin, the more I realized there was something so different about my relationship with him and the relationship I had with Bob. Bob had genuinely cared for me. I remembered the way he looked at me and the things he said. Bob loved me...*really* loved me, and I had never experienced that before. I really missed him and my life in California.

And then one day it hit me. I loved Bob! It was all starting to make sense. I *had* to come home to figure it out. I couldn't wait one more minute to talk to him. *What would he think? Would he take me back?* It had been ten months since I had seen him and six months since I had written him that letter. *Had he moved on?* I called his house a couple of times and finally reached him at work. Our conversation was very intense and stressful.

"I want to come back," I told him.

"Why? What's changed since the letter you wrote me?"

"I miss you," I said, choking back tears. "And I want to be with you."

"I'm seeing someone else," he said matter of factly. "After I got your letter, I thought I would never see you again."

"Do you love her?" I asked. He was silent. When he couldn't answer my question, I told him I would give my notice at work and see him in two weeks.

I called my parents and told them I was quitting my job and going back to California to be with Bob. They were so excited because they liked him from the first time they met him. I didn't have any money saved, so they bought me my plane ticket. We met for lunch before I left, and I told them about my conversation with Bob and how he was dating someone else.

"What if it's too late? What if he's moved on?" I asked.

My dad looked at me and said, "Honey, if he ever really loved you, it won't be too late."

His words gave me hope.

The three hours I spent on the plane felt like an eternity. I couldn't wait to see him face to face, but I still didn't know if he was going to take me back. As soon as I got to my sister Kerry's house in California, I called him. I was going to tell him to come over in an hour, so I would have time to get ready, but before I could get the words out, he hung up and was there within minutes. When I heard his voice, my heart started pounding, and my knees became weak. I walked out into the living room and hugged him. We left the house so we could talk. Before we were out of the driveway, he stopped the car and kissed me. We both knew this was forever. I never looked back.

Six months later, Bob got down on one knee and asked me to marry him. I said yes. We got married almost one year from the day I got back. All of my sisters were in the wedding, and Kirk was the best man. The reception was held in his mom's backyard with flowers everywhere and floating hearts in the pool. It was an amazing day.

Kirk (left) and Bob (right) on our wedding day

A short time later, we bought a home close to his mom and brother. I couldn't believe we had our own home. I loved his family, and I loved my life. It was picture perfect...until six months later when the accident happened.

December 1, 1978 was a day I will never forget. Kirk was such a big part of our lives, especially Bob's. We saw him almost every day. Everyone who knew him loved him. He was so full of life, and now he was gone.

The four a.m. wake-up call was still ringing in my ears. People were coming in and out all day long expressing their sorrow. The silence was deafening at times. The crying was unbearable. My imagination was running wild with thoughts of how the accident happened. *Did he suffer? Did he know?* I had always had a hard time facing my own emotions, but this was about to put me over the edge. I tried not to cry, because I was afraid I wouldn't be able to stop. I wanted to comfort Bob, but at the same time I wanted to run from this nightmare. And then there was his mom. I knew Bob was concerned about her too, but his own grief was all he could handle.

I had never seen anyone grieve like Bob did for his brother. He shut down and didn't want to talk about it. At times it really scared me, but I had to be strong for both of us. I needed someone to talk to, so I started another Dear God diary and continued to write for the next two years. I constantly asked God to protect my family, especially my husband, because I couldn't bear to lose him. Once again, I didn't know if God was listening or if He even cared.

On August 10, 1980, we had our first son. The love that I felt for him was stronger than anything I had ever experienced. It was amazing. I stared at him in awe and couldn't believe I was a mom. It was more than I could have ever asked for. I was bursting with joy.

On Robby's first birthday, we had a party and invited everyone to come. My heart was so full that day, but my fears continued to haunt me. I couldn't shake the thoughts that had been there since Kirk's death. *What if I lost my husband? What if I lost my son? How would I be able to live without them?*

I went to my husband's aunt Sue for answers. I had heard her talk about God several times, so I thought maybe she could help me with my fears. I cried and told her how grateful I was for my life, but at the same time was so scared that something bad might happen. I told her I wanted to thank God, but I didn't know how to get to Him. She asked me if I had ever been to a Bible study. I didn't know what she was talking about. I knew what a Bible was, but I didn't know anyone studied it or even read it. She told me about a Bible study for young moms that I might like. *What do I have to lose?*

I didn't know what to expect when I got there. I had never left my son with anyone except his grandma, so dropping him off in the nursery was difficult for me. Everyone was so nice, and there was just something different about them. There was a peace they had that I didn't understand. They seemed *genuinely* happy. I didn't know where anything was in the Bible, and I couldn't understand what they were talking about in class, but they made me feel like I belonged. They were so glad that I was there. They prayed out loud, and they prayed for *me*. I loved hearing their prayers. I went back week after week for the next four months.

I was never sure about where I would go when I died, but I had always believed that I was probably good enough to get into heaven someday. On a scale of one to ten, I believed most days I was a five, six, or at best, a seven. I figured that should count for something. After all, I wasn't perfect, but who was? When I compared myself to others, I wasn't *that* bad, at least by my standards. However, through reading and studying the Bible, I learned that God had a completely different standard. He showed me what the truth was for the first time; there wasn't *anyone* who was good enough to get into heaven. Romans 3:12 says, "All have turned away from God; all have done wrong. No one does good, not even one."

> Can we boast, then, that we have done anything
> to be accepted by God? No, because our acquittal
> is not based on our good deeds. It is based on our
> faith. So we are made right with God through
> faith and not by obeying the law.
>
> Romans 3:27 (NLT)

No wonder I wasn't sure about where I was going when I died. I thought it depended on me! Some days I thought I would make it, and other days I wasn't so sure. I never felt accepted by God because I wasn't! "We are made right in God's sight when we trust in Jesus Christ to take away our sins. And we all can be saved in this same way, no matter who we are or what we have done" (Romans 3:22, NLT).

What a relief this news was! I needed to put my faith and trust in Jesus Christ alone. The reason I didn't feel good enough is because I would *never* be good enough. But God already knew that, so He provided a way out with a different plan.

> The law of Moses could not save us, because of
> our sinful nature. But God put into effect a dif-
> ferent plan to save us. He sent His own Son in a
> human body like ours, except that ours are sinful.
> God destroyed sin's control over us by giving His
> Son as a sacrifice for our sins.
>
> Romans 8:3 (NLT)

For God made Christ, who never sinned, to be the offering for our sin, so that we could be made right with God through Christ.

2 Corinthians 5:21 (NLT)

What I needed to do was accept this good news, admit that I was a sinner, ask for forgiveness, and believe that Jesus paid the penalty for my sins. So that's exactly what I did! I gave it all to Him. I gave Him my sin, my fear, and my guilt. He allowed me to give Him my past in exchange for His future—my filth for His righteousness. He took my past and erased it through His death on the cross. I would no longer look the same to God. I would now be hidden in His Son's righteousness, not standing bare in my own sin: "For you died when Christ died, and your real life is hidden with Christ in God" (Colossians 3:3, NLT).

I had always known that Jesus died on the cross, but now I knew that He died for *me!* I had never felt so free. Jesus said in John 8:32, "And you will know the truth, and the truth will set you free."

All this time I tried to add good works to my already sin-stained life. It didn't work. It would *never* work. The truth was that God had to give me a new heart. And that is what happened. I no longer had to strive to make Him love me. I now *knew* He did. This was the love I had been looking for all my life!

After all these years of "Dear God" diaries, something changed. Instead of writing to a God I didn't know, this is what I wrote...

February 18, 1982
New beginning...Oh, heavenly Father. I have become a Christian, one of Your children. I could never say that before. I love You more than ever.

Everything was different! I read in John 5:24, "I assure you, those who listen to My message and believe in God who sent Me have eternal life. They will never be condemned for their sins, but they have already passed from death into life." I had crossed over from death to life. I was a brand-new person. My life and thoughts were completely changed and because of my newfound faith in Christ, there was nothing I wanted more than to be obedient to Him. I now wanted to live a life of obedience to the Word of God instead of living the way I had all these years—for my own convenience and whatever was best for me.

I continued to go to Bible study every week and fell more in love with the Lord and His Word every day. The more I was in the Word, the more I found that the fears I had about losing someone close to me began to fade away. When I realized how wide, how long, how high, and how deep His love really was for me (Ephesians 3:18), and that He would never leave me nor forsake me (Hebrews 13:5), I finally felt at peace about the future knowing that anything that happened in my life, He would be right there with me.

I then started thinking about everyone in my life. I now had a concern for others and their relationship with God. The first person was my husband. We had been married over three years and had a great relationship. We loved each other deeply, but I knew he wasn't a Christian. We were now what the Bible called *unequally yoked:* we were two people, sharing one life, but going in opposite directions. I wanted to share the good news with him but didn't know how. *Would he accept it? Would he accept me?*

> In the same way, you wives must accept the authority of your husbands, even those who refuse to accept the Good News. Your godly lives will speak to them better than any words. They will be won over by watching your pure, godly behavior.
>
> 1 Peter 3:1–2 (NLT)

When I read this verse my eyes were opened. I knew that no matter what his reaction to me or this news was, I needed to love him unconditionally. I could not allow the fact that we were unequally yoked come between us as husband and wife. *How are we going to make it? We are so different now.* I struggled a lot in those early days. I became angry, mostly at myself for not being able to do the things I knew were right. I cried a lot and sought counsel from older, wiser women in the Lord. Aunt Sue was one of them, and she had become a mentor to me. One day as I was telling her about my frustrations, she asked me a very important question: "If Bob doesn't change at all from the way he is now until the day he dies, do you want to stay with him and make it work, or do you want to leave?" I knew she wasn't asking me this question as if to give me a choice. She already knew the answer.

> And if a Christian woman has a husband who is an unbeliever, and he is willing to continue living with her, she must not leave him. For the Christian wife brings holiness to her marriage… You wives must remember that your husbands might be converted because of you.
>
> 1 Corinthians 7:13–14a, 16a (NLT)

My heart was transformed when I read this. I realized the love I had for my husband up until this point had been very selfish and conditional. I was now more concerned about where he would end up for eternity than about him making me happy, and I wanted to share the truth with him more than I wanted to get my own way. This new love was so different. It was a supernatural love that comes from the One who *is* love, a love that gives and expects nothing in return. This was something I was not capable of before God's Spirit took up residence in me. I'm not saying that my motives were always pure or that I did everything perfectly. I had to keep reminding myself that I could be content in any circumstance with God's help: "For I can do everything with the help of Christ who gives me the strength I need" (Philippians 4:13, NLT).

Since that time, we have had two more sons, and we will be celebrating thirty-three years of marriage this year! By the grace of God and the mighty power of His Word, the love I have for my husband is even stronger today than it was all those years ago.

Besides my husband, there was also my immediate family that I was concerned about. I wanted them to know and understand the gospel message—the good news—"...that Christ died for our sins, just as the Scriptures said. He was buried, and He was raised from the dead on the third day...Christ was raised first; then when Christ comes back, all His people will be raised." (1 Corinthians 15:3–4, 23 NLT).

I wanted them to have the faith that I had. I kept journaling and praying for God to change them all. What a comfort it was to really know for the first time that God was hearing my prayers and would answer them.

And we can be confident that He will listen to us whenever we ask Him for anything in line with His will. And if we know He is listening when we make our requests, we can be sure that He will give us what we ask for.

1 John 5:14–15 (NLT)

My life drastically changed twenty-nine years ago. I often shudder to think of where I was headed before the Lord poured out His grace and mercy on me. I am still journaling and thanking God every day for giving me life for death and pardon for condemnation. There is no greater joy in my life than to sit in the quiet, secure, holy, and intimate presence of my Lord and Savior, Jesus Christ. To Him be all the glory…

Note from Lori

It wasn't until eleven years after I came to know the Lord that God began to save my sisters one by one. I remember talking to my three sisters and two sisters-in-law through the years and praying for ways to share with them about the Lord. I talked to my little sister, Barb, a lot about the struggles she was having in her marriage. I knew that if she became a Christian, she would fall in love with Jesus like I did. I spoke with her a couple of times about my relationship with Him, but she couldn't understand it: "But people who aren't Christians can't understand these truths from God's Spirit. It all sounds foolish to them because only those who have the Spirit can understand what the Spirit means" (1 Corinthians 2:14, NLT).

In June of 1993, Barb called and said she wanted to come out and visit. She said she was tired of her life and the way things were. As soon as I hung up, I called around to see if there was a Christian conference that weekend that we could go to. I will let her tell the story. She does a much better job.

Heart of Stone: Barb's Story

> I will give them an undivided heart and put a
> new spirit in them; I will remove from them their
> heart of stone and give them a heart of flesh.
>
> Ezekiel 11:19 (NIV)

As a little girl, I often wondered who I would marry. I had fairy-tale dreams of my wedding day and what it would be like. In fact, it was not uncommon for me and my sisters to play dress-up and pretend to be blushing brides on our wedding day. Despite all of my imaginative play, I was ill-prepared when my *special day* actually arrived. My wedding day was nothing like the dreams I had as a little girl but was more of a nightmare to me. I desperately wanted out of my marriage before it even began.

It was May 1, 1982. My mom was helping me put on my wedding veil when she asked me, "Why are you marrying Denny?" Without hesitation I quickly responded, "Because I already sent out the invitations, and it's too late." Unfortunately, it wasn't a joke, and by the sad look on my mom's face, she knew I wasn't kidding. I would have rather been anywhere in the world than where I was standing at that very moment. I had grown so bitter over the past year and a half since meeting Denny. I resented him for so many reasons—actually—for *every* reason I could think of, and I couldn't believe I was going to be walking down the aisle to become Mrs. Denny Pagel.

You're probably wondering how I got to the point of marrying a man I resented—even hated—instead of marrying my "best friend" like so many married couples typically put it. You're probably wondering why I didn't just put on my running shoes and, well, run! Here's my answer: I have no idea! I have no idea what was going through my mind during that point of my life or why I didn't run, because I know I wanted to. But looking back today, I know that it was *all* for God's glory. I hope as you read my story the only thing you remember is how amazing God is and how nothing is too difficult for Him: "Behold, I am the Lord, the God of all flesh; is anything too difficult for Me?" (Jeremiah 32:27, NASB).

Whenever I think about my testimony and God's work in my life, I am in awe of the power of His grace. The longer I walk with Him, the more I realize how utterly lost I was. When you finish reading my story, I don't think you will disagree with me.

Just to give you a little background, there are six kids in our family. I won't say who is the oldest (Kerry), but I was the fourth-born, which granted me the title of "the oldest of the youngest." I didn't particularly like that role because I was confused about whether I should play with my younger siblings and be a kid like them, or if I should hang out with the older ones and be disobedient like them. So, I decided to do a little of both.

Before long, I became my own authority, and no one could tell me what to do, not my parents or my teachers, not my coaches or bosses, and definitely not my future husband. (Okay, so I didn't have any coaches; the only sport I competed in was rebelling). "Doing wickedness is like sport to a fool…" (Proverbs 10:23, NASB).

We didn't have a lot of material things, so when I entered into public school for the first time as a freshman, I became envious of what my friends had. I had been wearing a school uniform all through grade school and didn't realize that my meager wardrobe, which consisted of a handful of items, would not cut it if I was going to fit in with my peers. I knew we didn't have the resources to buy the things I wanted, and I didn't have a job, so I began to steal, even from the store where my mom was employed. I *never* got caught, and

I *never* felt guilty; I told myself that I deserved it. By the time I was in high school, my friends and I would fill up the back seats of our cars with clothing, jewelry, shoes, or anything else we wanted from the local stores in our small town.

When graduation day came, no one was happier than I was to be leaving high school. I had big plans to move out to California and be on my own, until my dad came in my room one night and asked me if I would consider going to an all-girls trade school in Omaha, Nebraska. He knew that one of my best friends was going there, and he thought it would be a good fit for me. Looking back, I'm pretty sure he wanted to protect me from myself. I wasn't crazy about the idea, but since it was only a twelve-month commitment, I decided to take his advice and go.

The day I moved into the dorm, my new roommates and I immediately hit it off...well, okay...hit it off once we broke our first rule of the school and smoked cigarettes together in our *non-smoking* dorm room. Before long, we began to go to the bars every weekend together. Since we had a ten p.m. curfew, we had to find a way to get into the dorm after hours. We did...but got caught more times than we succeeded. We definitely made sure the resident assistant had something to do.

After graduating, I moved into an apartment complex with some of my roommates from school. It was not unusual for us to begin our Friday nights with our own case of beer and then finish off the night with at least a dozen shots, only to begin again on Saturday morning. Some of us also began smoking pot and taking speed. Our partying became an everyday event. I don't know how my hundred-and-fifteen-pound frame withstood the daily consumption of alcohol and drugs.

At some point, I grew bored and decided to make a drastic change and quit partying altogether. I sold almost everything I owned, threw away my cigarettes, packed my clothes, and with fifty dollars in my pocket, decided to move to Southern California, where I had always dreamed of living. My two older sisters, Kerry and Lori, had been living there for several years, so I called and told them I was coming there to live. But after only six months in the California sun, I decided to move back to the Midwest and back in with my parents. Oh, lucky them! I can't imagine what they must have thought when they got that call from me. It was probably the first time they had considered leaving Nebraska.

I wasn't home too long before my mom told me I needed to keep my room clean if I was going to live at home. *What? Rules? Seriously? Not gonna happen.* I didn't have a clue how I could afford to live on my own. I decided to ask my little sister, Ellen, who was only seventeen and not even graduated from high school yet, if she would move into an apartment with me. I thought my parents would never go for it, but they did and even helped Ellen pay her half of the deposit. Ellen was so excited about moving into her first apartment with me, but that didn't last long. She had no idea what kind of a roommate I would be.

Both of us had full-time jobs, and whenever I ran out of money, which was quite often, I would call our little hometown bank and say that I was Ellen and ask them to transfer *her* money into *my* account. Whenever she discovered that her account was missing funds, she would always call me and ask if I took it. I remember getting so angry with her and telling her she was being so selfish for not wanting to help me out. The argument didn't end until *she* apologized to me. She *was* the little sister after all, and she owed me, right? In my mind, everyone did. This truly was my warped way of thinking. I began hanging out with my old friends again and went right back into the party scene. We had unlimited supplies of cocaine and valium, and many nights we didn't stop until it was gone. If that wasn't enough, I took speed every morning before going to work. I could hardly wait for the lunch hour, so I could go home and smoke pot and then get back to work again. As soon as I got off work, it was home to change and off to party some more.

Throughout all of this, I would attend church almost every Sunday because that's what I was taught. I remember one Sunday thinking about how proud

God must be that I was willing to get up early and go to church after being out all night. I was living out my single life with basically no authority, or at least none that I acknowledged; I had all the drugs and alcohol I wanted, an apartment, a job, and free access to my sister's bank account. It just couldn't get any better, right? But I did find out that it *could* get worse.

It was Friday, definitely my favorite day of the week. My boss announced that he was going over to our company's weekly afternoon get-together, which I chose *never* to attend. It just wasn't cool to hang out with the people I worked with. But when the other girls in my office asked me if I wanted to go, for some reason, I went this time. When I got there, I ended up sitting by Denny. He was the manager in the Iowa branch, and I was a secretary in the Nebraska branch. Everyone loved working for Denny and had a great deal of respect for him. I was somewhat intimidated by him because he was my boss's boss, so I never said much to him before this night. Once we began talking, we didn't quit. It was as if no one else was there. I knew that he was in the process of getting a divorce, but by the end of the night, none of that mattered. I was smitten, and I couldn't wait to see him again.

We talked on the phone that week, and I was so excited when he asked me out. Denny was so different than anyone I had ever dated. He actually *had* a job, and he was successful at what he did. The thing that

I was drawn to right away was that he seemed to be aware that there was a future ahead. Imagine that! I pretty much lived each day as it came, with no thought to the future, and so did everyone else I hung out with. Denny was mature and appeared to be confident about life in every way. He was, to put it another way, everything I was not.

On our first date, I found out that his impending divorce was his *second*, not his first, and that he also had a ten-year-old son. Red flag? Nah. What? Divorce? Kid? Divorce again? Did he say that? Houston, we may have a problem. I used all of my critical thinking skills to carefully weigh this decision for at least two seconds before I removed all red flags in my mind and decided all systems were go. I was crazy about him from the start and decided to overlook his speckled past. Wow, so generous of me, don't you think? Within two months, I moved in with him, and almost immediately our relationship began to crumble.

The move from my apartment to his was not a decision we consciously made but just happened slowly over time. I didn't have much in the way of possessions, so little by little I brought my clothes over until I was completely moved in. I was twenty-two years old and was not used to living with any type of authority figure, so one day when I was heading out the door to go shopping, I was surprised when Denny stopped me.

"Where are you going?" he asked.

"Are you kidding? Why do you want to know? It's none of your business!" I scowled.

What have I gotten myself into? Who does he think he is asking me where I'm going? I still remember the look of disbelief and question on his face right before I stormed out the door. I was not about to let anyone control me.

I had stopped hanging out with my friends since meeting Denny because he really wasn't into partying other than drinking, and I began to resent ever meeting him. I missed my carefree single life. Several months after we moved in together, Denny got a job in Omaha and asked me to go with him. I needed some time to think, so I moved back to my old apartment with my sister and her new roommate. I knew I couldn't stay with my sister much longer, and I wanted to quit my job anyway, so I decided to move to Omaha. *Who knows? Maybe the move to a new city might help our relationship.*

The next year in Omaha went from bad to worse. Denny traveled from Monday to Friday, so I stayed out most nights with my friends and coworkers and began smoking pot again. Denny was so disillusioned. But as much as he hated it, he was desperate for us to get along, so he began smoking with me. It didn't help. Whenever we were together, we were either drinking or fighting or both.

Right in the middle of all of this, Denny asked me to marry him. I really didn't know why he would, given our situation, but I figured after two failed marriages, he didn't want to fail again. Maybe this was all he knew when it came to relationships. Or maybe he just wasn't that bright. At this point, I was banking on the latter.

I still remember the day he was planning to pop the question. He asked me to go to a dinner theatre the week before. All week long he was acting strange—okay, stranger than usual—and I figured he was going to ask me to marry him. I remember thinking, *He can't even ask me to marry him without me figuring it out.* That just added to the list of loser qualities that I despised about him.

Just as I thought, Denny asked me to marry him that night, and even though I said "yes," everything inside me was yelling "no!" When I woke up the next day, I was numb. I had been with Denny for a year and a half, and I realized I had forgotten what it felt like to be happy. I couldn't believe that we were going to become husband and wife. I didn't think I could be more depressed until Denny asked me right away that morning if we could pick a date. *Oh, wow. Pick a date? I'm still grieving over the proposal, and I have to pick a date already?*

I was angry and immediately asked him if May first was on a Saturday.

He said, "Yeah, why?"

I said, "Because isn't May Day a distress call, like *Help! Help! Mayday, mayday?*"

He looked at me and in a questioning tone said, "Yeaaahh?"

"Okay," I said, "then that's the *perfect* date for our wedding day!"

Instead of upsetting him, which is what I was after, he simply and matter-of-factly said, "Okay, May first it is!"

Wow! Is he for real?

As our wedding day got closer, our fights became more intense. One night I was so angry at him I slammed my hand into our bedroom window and almost severed the tendons in my right hand. We went to one marriage counselor after another. We were told by several of them that we should not get married. *Really? Do ya think?* But, no matter what anyone said, we proceeded to move forward.

The day I went to look at wedding dresses was not the most memorable, but for some reason I've never forgotten it either. I didn't tell anyone I was going. I went by myself, tried on one dress, paid for it, drove home, and hung it in the closet. It was nothing short of sad.

Our wedding day, the honeymoon, and the days and months following were spent trying to convince myself and everyone else that everything was okay. I never wanted anyone to know about our problems, but once in a while I would call my older sister, Lori, and talk to her about it. I figured she lived far enough away that no one would find out. She tried to give me advice, but nothing seemed to help, not even going to church every week.

Denny said that one of the things that drew him to me in the very beginning was the devotion I had to my religion and to my church. But what he didn't know is that even though I claimed to have faith in God, it was not a saving faith from above. I had never heard about or received God's free gift of grace. I had religion, but I wasn't redeemed, and my life was evident of that.

About a year and a half into our marriage, I was talking to Lori again about our dying relationship, and just out of nowhere she started saying things like, "You need to focus on changing *you,* not Denny…you can't change Denny. Her counsel to me was strange, and no matter how bad I made Denny look, she kept bringing it back to me. She told me she was learning so many things about her marriage from the Bible. *The Bible? Since when do you read the Bible?* It was really annoying to me. I remember many times thinking, *What is up with her? I really need to find someone else to call.*

Our whole family was getting concerned that Lori might be in some sort of cult, so I decided to go out to California to see for myself. I spent five days with her, and she talked to me about her relationship with

Jesus. She said that since God saved her from her sin, she had so much peace. I was a little intrigued but a lot more confused. I didn't think her newfound happiness was genuine because no one is *that* happy. I tried to understand the things she was talking about, but everything fell on deaf ears (1 Corinthians 2:14). By the end of my stay with her, I thought she was really weird and had somewhat gone off the deep end. I figured she *really* must be missing something in her life to need God *that* much.

As I sat on the plane to go home, I began thinking, *God, please don't make me like Lori. Her whole life revolves around Jesus, and even You wouldn't want me to be like that, would You?* When I got home, I told everyone that I didn't think she was in a cult, but she was definitely a Jesus freak of some kind. Even though I didn't like the way she gave me advice from the Bible, I would still call her from time to time and ask for help because I didn't want anyone else to know about my failing marriage with Denny. I also figured that if anyone was going to pray for me every day it would be her, because that's all she did anyway!

In 1984, I found out that I was pregnant with our first child. I kept it from Denny for two weeks until the night before he was leaving on a business trip because I didn't want to have to celebrate and act happy together. I continued to party during my pregnancy, and after our first son was born, we were transferred to Lincoln, Nebraska. I didn't want to leave Omaha, but I thought this might be a chance for a fresh start for us: a new baby, a new town, and a new job for Denny that did not require much travel. The best part was that I knew my best friend from high school lived there, and I couldn't wait to meet up with her and go to the bars.

The first day after we got all settled in, I called her. Cheryl's son answered and said she was at a Bible study. I started laughing and then told him to have her call me when she got home. She called the next day, and after she told me all about her Bible study, she invited me to come with her the following week. I decided to go because I figured it would be a way to be around her and meet other women in my new town.

When we got there, everyone was giving me hugs and it felt really strange. After we sat down, they all began singing. *Wow, are they kidding? Who sings in their house?* They prayed and talked about the Lord, and I just sat and listened. By the end of the study, I didn't mind the women, and I liked being with Cheryl, so I went a couple more times.

After several years in Lincoln, we were transferred to Watertown, South Dakota. Even though it wasn't Denny's fault, I was still upset with him. *What else is new?* I loved Lincoln, and the last place I wanted to go was Watertown, South Dakota. I went kicking and screaming, but it didn't take long before I began finding friends in Watertown that would party with me.

We went dancing a lot, and even if Denny was with me, or *especially* if he was with me, I danced with other guys, sometimes the whole night. Denny knew there was nothing he could do to change me. The more he fought with me about it, the more I continued in my rebellion.

I started out almost every day smoking pot before feeding the kids breakfast, and I would get high right before Denny came home from work, so I could stand being around him. It didn't work. Every time I heard the garage door open at the end of the day, I would literally cringe. I would go days without looking at him, and one time didn't even know he had been growing a beard for two weeks. Denny and I were so desperate for answers, but we always seemed to come to a dead end no matter what we did.

After about six months in Watertown, I decided to look for a Bible study like the one I went to in Lincoln. When I couldn't find one, I decided to start my own. Oh, boy! I couldn't wait to tell Lori about it. I knew she would be so excited, but I was wrong. When I told her, she didn't say a word. *Hello?*

Then she asked, "Who's going to lead it?"

With excitement in my voice, I said, "*I* am! Isn't that awesome?"

Silence again.

What is wrong with her? I told Denny that night that I couldn't figure out why Lori acted so strange.

I remember telling him, "You would think she would be happy for me because she goes to Bible studies too. She is so strange!" But Lori knew that I was the *last* person who should be leading a Bible study.

The next day, I began calling some of my friends to see if they wanted to do a Bible study with me. Before the end of the day, there was about seven of us ready to begin. I couldn't wait! Our Bible study was a little different than the one I went to in Lincoln. We *definitely* didn't sing, and we rarely opened our Bibles, if ever. We never prayed, because why would we? We drank beer and wine coolers and...well...socialized! Some of the husbands named our group the BBB—Bibles, Broads, and Booze! But I was so proud of my little group that I had started, and everyone loved it. It was the highlight of our week. We talked about the things going on in our town and had a great time together.

We had been in Watertown about two years when Denny and I were invited to join a neighborhood Bible study with five other couples. The topic was parenting, and the only reason I considered going was because we had three boys by then and really needed help with parenting. Denny didn't want to go, but he reluctantly agreed to go in order to keep peace. Although we didn't know it at the time, the leaders were actually born-again Christians who had a burden for their unsaved neighbors. There were six couples including the leaders, and it was a really fun group.

One night, I said to Denny, "Why do Mike and Karen keep saying Jesus has to be number one in our lives? That is *so* weird. What does that mean? I mean… I think He is number one to us, right?"

Denny just shrugged his shoulders and said, "I guess…I don't know….yeah?"

We were clueless.

Being in a study with other couples should have been a good thing for us, but I began coveting their relationships. I would have rather been married to anyone else in that group than Denny. Some nights we would talk about wanting a better relationship, but we were lost as to how to go about it. We continued to seek out counseling and even marriage conferences, but nothing helped. We would be happy sometimes for maybe a week or so and have a little hope, and then *crash,* right back to where we were. We worked hard to look good to those around us, and might have fooled many people, but behind closed doors, we were a mess.

One day I decided I was done pretending. I couldn't take our marriage anymore. I spent the entire day rehearsing in my mind what I wanted to say to Denny. When he got home from work, I asked him if he would take our three boys downstairs so we could talk. He thought I was going to ask for a divorce, but it was much worse—something he didn't expect at all.

Minus the many expletives, I said to him, "Denny, I am *never* going to ask you for a divorce because that's something I don't believe in, but I am *never* going to love you either. I hate you more than anyone in this world! *You* can divorce me if you want, and I will gladly give it to you because you make me want to vomit. In fact, I want you to know that I pray daily that you will come home and tell me you are having an affair, or that you want out. And whenever I hear a knock at the door, I pray that it is the highway patrol coming to tell me that you have been in a fatal accident because I wish you were dead—a*nything* to get out of this marriage. So, as of today, I'm detaching myself from you. I don't care how you feel or what you think, and I'm going to become just like you—dead! Don't expect anything from me, and I will expect nothing from you!"

The color drained from his face, and he didn't say a word. He was devastated, and I had accomplished what I set out to do—hurt him to the very core. I was cheering inside and felt like a huge weight had been lifted. I was finally free. Or so I thought...

For the next two months, we were civil to each other, but most nights I would take our boys out to eat before Denny came home, so we weren't there when he arrived. We had become roommates—not husband and wife—and Denny couldn't figure out what to do.

He prayed all the time asking God for help, but he never got an answer. The harder he tried to be a good husband, the more I loathed him. I kept Denny at a comfortable distance and didn't care to be any kind of wife. Our marriage was empty and void of love. We had no order in our home and no hope for a future. It had been ten long years, and we were both exhausted from the nothingness in our marriage. Denny decided to attend an outpatient self-help program, which, like every other worldly thing we tried, bombed two weeks after he came home. *So now what?*

Right around this time, I began to experience severe pain in my back and neck. I went to a physical therapist, and by the end of my appointment with him, I could barely move. He definitely made things worse, but I kept hoping it would just go away. I had no idea what was wrong, but after a few more days of sitting in a chair, I decided to go to a regular doctor, who prescribed some very strong pain killers and anti-inflammatory medicine. They didn't even touch the pain searing through my neck. I remember crying every day because I couldn't hold my boys. Denny was at a loss as to what to do and one day suggested I go to a chiropractor. I had never been to one before and felt hopeless that *anyone* could help at this point. But I was desperate. It had been ten days, and I hadn't been able to sleep in a bed the entire time, so I decided to go. After the doctor realized that I couldn't lay down on the table, he said, "I think you have a ruptured disc, and you have two choices: you can either have surgery or you can have surgery. Which one do you want?" I knew he was trying to make me laugh, but I started crying instead because someone finally knew what was wrong with me. He referred us to a neurosurgeon in Sioux Falls, South Dakota. Denny found someone to watch the boys, and we went to the hospital right away. We were both so relieved.

I ended up being in the hospital for eight days, and unless I had an occasional visitor, the only other thing I could do was watch television. All weekend long, there were documentaries on adoptions. I watched the programs every chance I got and began to wonder if *we* could do that. I knew after we had our third son that I would want more children, but since my boys were only six, four, and almost two years old, I hadn't really given it much thought yet.

It was finally Monday. I was looking forward to having my surgery so I could get back home. The surgery was a success, and after a few more days in the hospital, we went home. Within a few short months, I was back to my old routine.

I began sharing with Denny about the adoptions I had seen on television and wondered what he thought about adopting a baby. He was confused and asked me why we wouldn't just have our own. I told him I didn't know why we should have our own when there are so many babies out there who need to be adopted. I quickly told him not to say yes or no right away but to think about it and let me know. Within a few weeks, he told me he thought we should go for it. I was so excited, I almost kissed him. Just kidding. To this day, I'm pretty sure he was willing to do anything to bring peace between us.

I immediately began looking for adoption agencies and found three possibilities. Within a week, we had been accepted by one of them, and our dream of adoption began. Within only six short months, we adopted a little girl, and baby makes four. The whole process of bringing another child into our family did bring Denny and I closer together, but it didn't last long. We continued to go to the bars, had more fights, experienced more silent treatments and outbursts of anger, and Denny was at the end.

Since moving to Watertown, Denny knew that I had a strong desire to live in Sioux Falls. It was one of the bigger cities in South Dakota, and I loved going there to visit. He asked his boss for a transfer hoping that it might help our marriage. When his boss gave him the go ahead, we sold our house, quickly packed up everything, and moved to the city of our dreams. I knew I would miss my friends, but I was so excited for a fresh start. We found our dream home, a new church, new neighbors, and friends. Maybe this change of scenery was just what we needed.

Summertime was fast approaching, and the newness of our move had already worn off. One morning, I woke up and struggled to put one foot in front of the other. I stood frozen in our living room looking out the window at nothing. There seemed to be so much darkness all around me. It was like a thick blanket, and everywhere I turned, it was there. *What is wrong with me? Why can't I be happy? Why can't we be happy?* I was so down at this point, because I knew that we had come to the end of the *things* that we thought might help us. I was so filled with rage and bitterness because of our situation. I was angry at everyone and everything. It was the lowest of lows for me. I had driven several of my friends away, and I hadn't talked to my little sister, Ellen, in three years all because we had an argument that didn't go my way. I was tired of hiding who I really was from everyone, including my parents and my siblings. I had a heart filled with hatred, and I knew I couldn't live like this another day.

I called Lori and Kerry and told them I was coming out to California to visit. Knowing that Kerry was moving back to Nebraska in a week, Lori asked, "Why are you coming out?"

I told her, "I don't know why I'm coming out there, but I don't want to come back the same person."

I booked my flight and told Denny I was going to California to visit my sisters. He was not happy with my decision to go out there, but what was he going to do? Tell me not to go? *That's funny.* He took me to the airport, and when he pulled up, he began to get out. "Don't!" I yelled. "Don't you dare get out! I don't need your help!" My body shook in disgust as I slammed the door and walked into the airport. *Loser.* I was so relieved to get away from him and everything else that was bringing me down.

When I got to Lori's house, she said, "Guess where you and I are going on Friday night?"

"Just you and I? Where? The bars?" I asked her.

And with what I thought was a little *too* much excitement, she said, "Church!"

I looked at her and said, "What? Church? Why? Who goes to church on a Friday night?" *Oh boy, this is going to be fun.* I was not happy about it, but I figured we could just go out afterward. When we got there, I couldn't believe how many people were there.

I asked Lori why there were so many people at church on a Friday night, and I will never forget what she said, "They love it here!"

Wow. That's really strange.

I don't remember a lot of what the pastor said that night, but I remember him talking about end times and how the Lord would soon return for His people. At the end of the service, he called people down to the front. I asked Lori what they were all doing down there, and she said they were asking God for forgiveness for their sins so they could become Christians. *Become a Christian? Oh, well, that's not me. I'm already a Christian.*

The pastor began to pray but then stopped abruptly, and we all looked up. He said, "There is one more person who needs to come down here and repent and ask God to forgive them, and I'm not going to pray until they do." Everyone fell silent.

I looked at my sister and said, "I think that's me!"

She looked at me and said, "Really?"

I said, "Yeah, but I'm scared to go by myself." When she said she would go with me, that's all I needed to hear. I got up and ran to the front of the church. With tears pouring down my face, I cried out to God to forgive me of my sins and become the Lord and Savior of my life.

I had a joy come over me that I had never known, and the weight of my sin was lifted. I was in awe of God for the first time in my life. Before I walked out the doors of the church, my heart was flooded with love and all the past hatred and anger and bitterness had vanished. Before we went home that night, I told Lori I couldn't wait to see Denny. No one could question this was a God-given miracle. One minute I was sitting there with no thought about my sin or repentance or faith, and the next minute, I was running to Him for forgiveness. Without a doubt, God supernaturally gave me a new heart and brought me to faith in Jesus Christ, so I could repent and believe—something I could never do on my own. "But whenever anyone turns to the Lord, then the veil is taken away" (2 Corinthians 3:16–17, NLT).

On June 24, 1993, I fell in love with my Lord and Savior, Jesus Christ. That day, I heard and understood the message of the gospel. I finally saw my anger, hatred, and selfishness for what it was: sin against God and against others. For the first time, I had hope for change, and I soon found out it was a radical change from the inside out. I know that it was all of God, from start to finish, because I was certainly not seeking out a relationship with Him; I thought I already had one. I thought I *was* a believer, but I was fooled. I was nothing more than a make-believer. I didn't understand right away what had happened to me, but I soon figured out that I had a divine appointment with the Lord that night.

Shortly after we got home, the phone rang. It was Denny. I could hear the kids screaming in the background, and I asked him what he was doing. With an angry voice he asked, "What do you think I'm doing? I'm taking care of the kids while you're having fun with your sisters in California!"

Normally, I would have blasted him with some colorful words and hung up on him, but instead I quietly said, "Hey, why don't you put the kids down and call me back so we can talk."

Denny knew something was up when I didn't respond back in anger. It didn't take him more than five minutes, and the phone rang.

"So…uh…what are you guys doing?"

I didn't want to tell him a lot about what happened right then on the phone, so I told him I would talk to him when I got back the next day. I'm sure he was shocked when I added, "I can't wait to see you!"

Lori and I spent the rest of the night talking about the Lord. I asked her one question after another. I finally understood her passion and excitement over her relationship with Jesus. I was already so filled with love for Him I was coming out of my skin. It was the greatest high I had ever experienced!

As I sat in my seat on the plane, my mind was consumed with thoughts about Jesus and I wondered if anyone knew Him. I was rejoicing from the inside out, and I had a never-ending smile on my face. I realized that all my life, I had heard about God, but I had never seen Him for who He really was. "I had heard about You before, but now I have seen You with my own eyes" (Job 42:5, NLT).

As the plane landed, I could hardly sit still. I couldn't wait to see Denny and the kids. When I came off the plane, they were all standing there waiting for me. I walked over to Denny and gave him a kiss and a hug. I teared up and couldn't quit staring at him. I loved what I saw! To this day, Denny says that my eyes were soft and alive, and my voice was calm. He was expecting me to walk up and hug the *kids* and ignore *him,* so he was shocked that I even made eye contact with him. I could tell that his mind was flooded with questions. Even our seven-year-old son looked up at me at the airport and said, "Mom, what happened to you?"

Denny could hardly wait to get home so we could talk. As soon as our kids were in bed, I began to share with him about what happened on Friday night. I told him every detail, and explained how the hatred and anger and bitterness were gone before I even left the church and that I knew I was going to heaven now. I didn't know if he would understand anything I was saying, but I hardly stopped to breathe as I told my story.

He looked at me and said, "I want what you have, and I want to go to heaven. What do I need to do?"

I told him, "I'm not really sure, but I know that you need to ask Jesus to forgive you for your sins and surrender your life to Him."

Denny didn't hesitate. "I want to do that." So we went to our knees, held hands, and bowed our heads and prayed together. God changed Denny's heart that night, and he has never been the same. He is a new creation and is so in love with Jesus. To this day, I don't know anyone who is more grateful to His Savior or more passionate about the gospel message.

The next day, Denny was walking toward me in the hallway and asked, "Why haven't we ever heard the gospel before?"

I said, "I don't know. Maybe we did but just couldn't hear it."

As we stood there in the hallway talking, we instantly felt a love for each other that neither of us thought was possible. When God gave us new hearts, we fell passionately in love with Jesus, and then fell head over heels in love with each other for the first time. "We love, because He first loved us" (1 John 4:19, NASB). God transformed our hearts toward Him, and then He transformed our marriage. "And I will give them singleness of heart and put a new spirit within them. I will take away their hearts of stone and give them tender hearts instead" (Ezekiel 11:19, NLT).

Within the next few weeks, I told Denny I really wanted to go see Ellen. With his blessing (yes, you heard me right, I asked him for permission), I got in the car and drove to her house, which was seventy-five miles away. When I pulled up, she was sitting in her driveway with my dad and her new baby. I had never seen Ryan, so I couldn't wait to see him, but I was more excited about seeing Ellen. When she saw me, her mouth dropped open in disbelief. "What are you doing here?" I told her I just really wanted to see her. Right away she asked if I wanted to go inside to see Austin, her two-year-old son, whom I barely knew. We talked a mile a minute to each other and laughed at Austin, who was bouncing off the walls in excitement. It felt so good to be able to look at her and hug her and love her like I had never done before. To this day, we are not only sisters but best friends. God's grace is more than amazing.

A few months after we became believers, Denny and I were talking about our newfound love for Christ and each other. Prior to being saved, we did not understand the purpose of the cross because we didn't understand the gravity of our sin and that we had fallen short of God's glorious standard. We had no clue that we were in danger of slipping into hell, and the only way we could be spared from eternal separation from God was to have Him intervene in our lives so we could be born again. We were incapable of living the lives that God wills for us, so He did it *for* us by sending His Son.

It has been seventeen years since Denny and I were saved by God's amazing grace. Jesus is *more* than number one in our lives—He *is* our life. He is the center of our world and the center of our marriage. I never thought I would ever be able to respect or love Denny, much less look at him without disgust. But now, I can't get enough of him. We are not perfect by any means, but I can't wait to hear his footsteps coming in the door after work, and I continually pray that God will protect him wherever he goes. We cherish our time together as a couple, and as parents of five amazing kids, but mostly, as children of the most high God.

Denny and I in 2010

Our life now is evidence of the truth of how God can and does change His people, and not just for the better—but forever. Denny and I can't ever share our testimony without tears, because we are reminded of how God predestined us to adoption, redeemed us, and chose to lavish His great love and grace on us and make us right with Him through the cross.

He predestined us to adoption as sons through Jesus Christ to Himself, according to the kind intention of His will, to the praise of the glory of

His grace, which He freely bestowed on us in the Beloved. In Him we have redemption through His blood, the forgiveness of our trespasses, according to the riches of His grace which He lavished on us...

Ephesians 1:5–8 (NASB)

Note from Lori

In the summer of '95, two years after Barb and Denny's radical transformation, my brother Bob, my sister-in-law Shelly, and their two daughters made a trip to the West Coast. They went to Arizona first to visit Barb's family and then to California to stay with mine. Shelly had shared with Barb and I that she had started going to a Bible study in Kansas. We were both very excited and couldn't wait to talk to her. This is Shelly's story…

Captive to Fear:
Shelly's Story

The Spirit we received does not make us slaves
again to fear; it makes us children of God. With
that Spirit we cry out, "Father."

Romans 8:15 (NCV)

"Look! Look!" Sherry said with excitement as she
ran over to me. "Grandpa and I have two tickets to
ride the helicopter! They are going to take us up by
Mount Rushmore to see the Presidents' faces!"

"Yeah, yeah, whatever," I responded with no enthu-
siasm. My little sister had always been the risk-taker.
She was outgoing and feisty. I, on the other hand, was
more reserved and cautious. We had just gotten back
from the tram ride that had taken us way above the
trees and the tops of the hills. That was thrilling enough
for me, and I was glad to get back on the ground. But I

looked at her big, round, brown eyes and adorable smile and couldn't help wishing I was a little more like her.

My sister and I were in the Black Hills vacationing with my grandparents. We would spend at least a week with them every summer, but this was the first time they had taken us somewhere out of state. Sherry and I were inseparable. Being just twenty months apart, we did everything together. We played on the same softball teams each year and would do our hair together, putting it in pigtails or braids and even wearing matching ribbons. We had shared the same small bedroom with a double bed since we were little, and we would lie there almost every night and say our prayers together...*Now I lay me down to sleep... I pray the Lord my soul to keep...*then we would have a competition to see who could blow the most kisses to God.

This is our family...Sherry is on the left

School would be starting in a couple of weeks, and this was going to be a great way to end our summer. I was actually looking forward to school starting because we were both going to be majorettes for our junior high bands. I was in the ninth grade, and she was in seventh. We would be on the football field together at all the games and even be in the parades! We did have our moments, but for the most part we were best friends, and this trip was proving no different. We were having such a great time. The first couple of days we went sightseeing, toured lots of caves, and walked up the hills. We had gone into the gift shop to look for souvenirs when my sister announced that they were going on the helicopter ride. Grandma and I waited in line with them and took pictures as they were getting on the helicopter. Grandpa handed his billfold, car keys, and watch to Grandma. "Just in case we don't come back," he said with a smile.

There were five helicopters going out that day. Grandma and I stood there and watched as they took off. As soon as they were out of sight, we went into the gift shop again to wander around and wait for them to come back. It didn't seem like we had been there very long when, all of a sudden, one of the pilots came running in and told the manager that one of the helicopters had gone down in the hills. I held my breath as the helicopters came back one by one. As the fourth helicopter landed, my heart sank—it wasn't theirs. We still didn't know what happened or how bad it was. *Maybe they survived. Maybe they were just hurt.* The owner took another helicopter to find out where they had gone down. It seemed like forever before he came back. He walked into the gift shop where Grandma and I were waiting and, with a stern look and no emotion in his voice, he said, "They're all dead," and then walked straight into his office and closed the door. It felt as if all the blood drained from my body. I was devastated, numb, and confused, like it was all a bad dream. *Things like this don't happen to people like my sister and me.*

Right then, one of the ladies that worked there came over to us and asked if we needed to use the phone. Grandma looked at me and asked, "Do *you* want to call your mom?"

I just looked up at her, shrugged my shoulders, and said quietly, "Okay."

We went to the back office. My grandma picked up the phone and dialed the number slowly. She handed me the phone. "Grandma, I don't know what to say," I said, handing the phone back to her. My mom answered right away. When Grandma told my mom the news, I heard her scream and then drop the phone. The paramedics drove us back to our hotel and helped us pack our things. Grandma packed for Grandpa, and I packed for Sherry. *She's coming home, right?* I still couldn't believe this was happening.

Someone else drove us to another hotel in Rapid City, so we could wait for a family member to pick me up and drop off my uncle who would identify the bodies. As we waited in the room, we turned on the television only to find the news of the fatal helicopter crash. They reported that the gas gauge on the helicopter didn't work and that it had run out of gas on the way back. They believed they were crushed on impact and were killed instantly. I was sick to my stomach.

As I lay there that night waiting for my family to arrive, I couldn't sleep. I was so scared, and I couldn't get my thoughts to slow down. *What did she go through? Did she know they were crashing? Did she cry out for my mom or dad? Where was God in all of this? Did He care? How could He let this happen?*

As a child, I had always been fearful and carried worry around like it was my job. When we would go to the store with my mom, my little sister and baby brother would run around and play hide and seek. But I would stick close to my mom, not wanting to be lost. I was very needy and dependent. Even Sunday school was stressful to me. I enjoyed going, but when the bell would ring and the doors opened into the hallway, all I saw was a sea of people, *big* people, and I would think, *How are my mom and dad ever going to find me?* I don't know why, but I didn't like being separated from my family. And now my biggest fear was staring me right in the face.

It started becoming a little more real as I flew back home. I was looking out the window of the plane trying to see the hills and wondering where Sherry was. *Why isn't she with me?* I got off the plane and walked toward my dad with my suitcase in one hand and Sherry's in the other. Nothing seemed right. I felt lost and scared. The car ride home was eerily quiet.

When we got there, our house was full of family and friends. In a way it was comforting to have them there, but I just wanted to be alone. I hadn't really talked to anyone about it yet, because I didn't really know what to say. If I did say something, I was afraid it would make my mom cry. It was all a blur. My little brother Shane was only five years old and was oblivious to what was going on.

I helped pick out the clothes Sherry would be buried in and the songs to be sung at her funeral. I chose *Seasons in the Sun* by Terry Jacks and *Time in a Bottle* by Jim Croce. For those first few days I found myself just whimpering all the time. I couldn't seem to pull myself together. Sherry's funeral seemed so wrong; she was only twelve years old. I got to keep her little turquoise ring that she was wearing when she was killed. I still have it on a chain to this day.

The next day, we drove two and a half hours to my Grandpa's funeral. I was going through the motions, but none of it had really sunk in yet. Once we got back home, I remember walking in and thinking, *I just lost my best friend.* Her picture came out in the paper with the article about the crash. Two days later, a picture of our softball team was in the paper for winning the championship—it was like she was still alive. I just wanted to go back in time and make it turn out a different way. I was angry and feeling sorry for myself, thinking about how unfair it was that everyone else's life went on as usual, but ours had come to a halt and was changed forever.

Every night, we would sit in our living room reading cards from family and friends. Neighbors would stop by to visit and bring food. All of that was comforting, but all I wanted was to have my sister sitting next to me. It was difficult to be out and about with friends, because my mind would continually wander back to Sherry, but it was better than being alone.

God came to the forefront of my life that summer, but not in a good way. As a thirteen-year-old girl, I was wrestling with so many thoughts. *Maybe it should have been me.* I feared God, but not the way you are supposed to. I didn't trust Him. I wondered a lot about heaven and wondered if Sherry was there. I struggled so much with leaving her at the cemetery forty-five minutes away in the cold ground. Many nights, I wondered why God didn't just appear to me so He could tell me exactly what I wanted to hear. I tried to walk a fine line with Him—not too close—but not too far from Him either. I didn't want Him to hurt me again. I felt so vulnerable, and I didn't want to worry or wonder anymore. I always knew things like this happened, but it wasn't supposed to happen to *our* family. Little did I know, this would keep me pursuing my questions and lead me to the One who had the answers.

School started and it occupied my time and mind. I tried to stay busy so I didn't have to feel the loss. One of the best things that happened that year was in English class. Our teacher required us to come in and journal every morning in our spirals. That whole year I filled up those pages with thoughts about my sister and what I was going through. My mom and dad were just going through the motions and struggling to keep things together. They were both trying to deal with their own grief, so I didn't want to burden them with mine. The teacher told us that if we wanted her to answer us back, we were to leave our spirals on her desk when we were done. Every single day I would leave my spiral on her desk, and every day I would get it back. Journaling helped me to release a lot of the feelings I was having at the time. I don't know what I would have done without it.

For two years, my downstairs bedroom was a shrine to my sister. The walls were decorated with ribbons from the flowers on her casket and the newspaper articles about the helicopter crash. My room was a place that I could go and just be alone with my thoughts. I remember writing letters to Sherry often.

I'd go out in the driveway in the back of our house and burn them, thinking somehow they would reach God and He would give Sherry the message.

I made it through high school with God in and out of my thoughts; the distant reality of Him hovered around me. I had wonderful friends who listened to my story and helped carry me through and were there when I needed them the most. What people saw of me on the outside was not what was going on in the inside. I spent most of my time with my boyfriend, Bob, and lots of friends doing activities. I would drink occasionally, sometimes to the point of getting intoxicated. It was those times that I felt free from the worries and pain and the burden of always trying to hold it together. Alcohol became my way of escaping.

After graduation, it was time for me to leave home and enter the world of college. A few weeks before I was ready to leave, we found out my dad needed to have open-heart surgery. The fear and emptiness consumed me again. *Couldn't God pick on someone else?* We loaded up Bob's car with all of my stuff, and he took me to college. Leaving my parents for the first time, and not knowing if my dad would make it through surgery in a few weeks, I found myself quietly crying all the way there.

When I got there, I didn't know anyone. After Labor Day, my roommate didn't come back to school, so I had more alone time than I wanted—time I spent wondering and worrying about my family. Feelings of loneliness, separation, fear, and anxiety consumed me.

I went home the day before my dad's surgery. I didn't want my dad to die, so that night I sat at the kitchen counter and started making deals with God. It went something like this: *If You will just let my dad live, then I will start going to church.* My dad came through with just a few complications, and I figured God had heard me. I never did follow through with my end of the deal.

I've heard that the death of a child can either bring a family closer together or tear it apart. Unfortunately, it was the latter for us. It was very difficult to watch my parents struggling in their marriage. Over and over I wondered, *Why is this happening to my family?* Nothing was taking away the fear or filling the emptiness.

In the meantime, my relationship with Bob was very unstable. We drank a lot, and I depended on him to meet all of my needs. I would do anything to stay with him because I needed someone to take care of me. He probably stayed with me out of guilt or fear that I'd totally fall apart if he broke up with me.

My parents divorced the summer of my junior year in college, and I felt abandoned. No matter how young or old you are, there is a huge loss when your parents divorce. *How can I reach out to them? How can I support them when I am going through my own grief?* Did God not know that I couldn't deal with any more losses? I felt as though He had *completely* abandoned me now. I was desperate for some guidance and stability, but I didn't know where to turn.

After graduating from college, I got my first apartment and my first teaching job. My relationship with Bob was on again, off again. I wanted to get married, but he wouldn't commit. We ended up parting ways a couple of times, and I thought I was losing it.

A few months after our most recent breakup, Bob and I ran into each other at a bar. We picked up right where we left off, except for one thing. This time, we knew that the only way we could stay with each other would be to commit. I asked him right then and there to marry me, and he said yes. I quickly asked, "Then will we go get the ring tomorrow?" I was wise enough by now to know that I better not waste any time or he would change his mind, so I immediately began making plans. We set the date and reserved the church. I was sure that getting married would be the answer to everything and would surely take care of my emptiness.

Sometime during this time, my mom had accepted Jesus Christ as her Lord and Savior. She tried to talk to me and Bob about it, only to be made fun of. She suggested that before we get married we should go through counseling. We both agreed to do that and also decided that we needed to eliminate alcohol in our lives. It was one of the best decisions we ever made.

After we were married, we never attended church, but every now and then I was reminded about life and death as my other grandpa, my cousin, and my college roommate passed away. God had taken loved ones again, leaving me scared and questioning life. At the same time, I was aware that God was also the giver of life. He blessed us with two adorable daughters, Kayla and Jenna.

A few months after Jenna was born, we relocated to Louisville, Kentucky, so Bob could start a new job, which involved studying many hours and taking exams. I was teaching children with behavior disorders full time, so we had a young lady come to the house and watch the girls during the day. It was the best of times and the worst of times, and we were all we had.

We were far away from home with what seemed like insurmountable responsibilities. By this time, I had made up my own religion for my own satisfaction. I decided I didn't need an organized religion that just wanted my money. I refused to think that there was a hell or a devil and thought, *All good people go to heaven and live happily ever after, right?*

The following summer, I was overwhelmed with depression and anxiety. One of my friends suggested a place for me to receive counseling. At the time, it helped me deal with some of the pain of my losses, but the relief I felt didn't last. I continued to struggle to pull myself together. Then, after three years of Southern living, we were both able to get jobs in Kansas City and move closer to home.

We had been living in Kansas City for about a year when a friend asked if I wanted to be in a Bible study. I was a bit confused because we both swore like sailors, so I wondered if I would have to clean up my act. I hesitated because I was afraid of what I was getting myself into, but I figured maybe I could fake it and still look like a good person. I made sure they all knew that I had my own beliefs, and I was sticking to them. I had no idea what was in store for me.

Week after week, as I read and answered the questions in the workbook, I started finding out the truth of who God really was. One week as I was doing my study, I came across John 3:16, Titus 3:5–7, and Ephesians 2:8–9.

> For God so loved the world, that He gave His only begotten Son, that whoever believes in Him shall not perish, but have eternal life.
>
> John 3:16 (NASB)

> He saved us, not on the basis of deeds which we have done in righteousness, but according to His mercy, by the washing of regeneration and renewing by the Holy Spirit, whom He poured out upon us richly through Jesus Christ our Savior, so that being justified by His grace we

would be made heirs according to the hope of eternal life.

Titus 3:5–7 (NASB)

For by grace you have been saved through faith; and that not of yourselves, it is the gift of God; not as a result of works, so that no one may boast.

Ephesians 2:8–9 (NASB)

I loved what I was reading and wanted to know more about God. I continued to read, and there on another page, I saw a verse about being born again. I had heard that term before, but I wanted nothing to do with it because I always thought it meant I would be expected to stand on the street corner and hand out pamphlets. I wasn't aware that Jesus said a person *had* to be born again in order to go to heaven.

Jesus answered and said to him, "Truly, truly, I say to you, unless one is born again he cannot see the kingdom of God." Nicodemus said to Him, "How can a man be born when he is old? He cannot enter a second time into his mother's womb and be born, can he?" Jesus answered, "Truly, truly, I say to you, unless one is born of water and the Spirit he cannot enter into the kingdom of God. That which is born of the flesh is flesh, and that which is born of the Spirit is spirit. Do not be amazed that I said to you, 'You must be born again.'"

John 3:3–7 (NASB)

Later that summer, we took a family trip to Arizona and California to see Bob's sisters and their families. I had shared with them that I was doing a neighborhood Bible study, and boy did they jump on that. We went to Arizona first where we stayed with Barb and Denny.

I remember going to church with them on Sunday. Their pastor mentioned something about being saved. *Saved? Saved from what?* I was confused. I decided to ask them what he meant when we got home.

"What did your pastor mean when he said that a person needs to be *saved?*"

"Being saved means that you have been given a new heart and have accepted the free gift of salvation," Barb answered. "The Bible calls it being born again. Do you know what it means to be born again?"

"I heard about it in my Bible study before and prayed with my teacher to receive Christ, but what does it mean?" I asked.

Denny responded by saying, "Jesus said in order for you to go to heaven, you must be born again. A person who is born again is someone who has placed his faith and trust in what Jesus has done on the cross.

In other words, he fully trusts that Jesus's death on the cross has paid the price for his sins."

Then Barb asked, "Do you believe that? Do you believe that Jesus Christ died on the cross, was buried, and rose again?"

"Yes!" I exclaimed.

She asked if they could pray for me, so we all held hands and prayed.

We then went to California to see his other sister, Lori, and her family. Lori and I talked a lot about the Lord and being born again. She told me about grace and how it was a gift from God, and I was so excited about what I was learning. The next night, we went to a baseball game at Angel Stadium. After the game, the stadium went dark, and the fireworks started. As I sat in awe of the sparkles in the sky above us, I felt like God was there.

Our vacation came to an end, and we went back home. The next morning, I was working on my Bible study for the upcoming week. I was almost done with my lesson when I came across the gospel message in a prayer: *Heavenly Father, I come to You in prayer asking for forgiveness of my sins. I confess with my mouth and believe with my heart that Jesus died on the cross that I might be forgiven and have eternal life. I realize that I am unable to come to You on my own and that I need a Savior. Jesus, thank you for dying on the cross for my sins and providing salvation for me. Please come into my life and be my personal Lord and Savior. In Jesus's name, amen.*

My heart was pounding. God sent His Son to die for *my* personal sins. It was all starting to make sense. I needed His forgiveness. I began to pray and ask God to forgive me and be the Lord of my life. On July 9, 1995, there at my dining room table, God changed my heart, and I knew that I was a child of God, saved by His grace and heaven bound. "These things I have written to you who believe in the name of the Son of God, so that you may know that you have eternal life" (1 John 5:13, NASB).

Week after week, I became more passionate about God and His Word. The more I was in the Word, the more I became aware of all of the unsaved people in my family and began to pray for them. I started attending a Moms-in-Touch prayer group, and I'll never forget the first time hearing women I barely knew praying their hearts out for God to save my two daughters. I was blessed in so many ways with all of these ladies in my life.

One of the things I didn't know at the time was that my mom, who had been living in Kansas City for a few years, had moved there specifically to witness to our family, so we could come to know the Lord. When she was sure that I was saved, her mission was accomplished, and she decided to move back to our hometown in Nebraska to show the love of God to my brother and his wife. I am so appreciative of the seeds my mom planted in my life, along with many others whom God used to share the gospel with me.

I continued to attend my Bible study and Moms-in-Touch and met so many awesome Christian women, many of whom lived right in my neighborhood. Several years later, my part-time teaching assignment was switched to a different school with a different schedule. Instead of mornings, I would be working in the afternoons. *Oh no!* I thought. My Bible study and prayer group were in the afternoons. *I'll have to do everything on my own now!* I was so disappointed! For the next three years, I tried to do it on my own but was very unsuccessful. There was no consistency in the Word, and there was no connection or accountability with other women.

One Sunday, I heard about a study at our church called, "Women at the Well." I didn't think I had time for a Bible study or small group at that time, so I began to pray about it. God amazed me again. When I made a phone call to the gal in charge, she said they had a group on Monday evenings, and I even knew the leader. Mondays ended up being perfect for me, and it was an awesome study. I loved the time I spent learning about the Lord. Today, I mentor a young lady and co-lead a small group.

As I look back, I realize that the old me was always searching for something to relieve my fears and fill the emptiness inside. Since I have come to know Jesus, I have found what I was searching for, and I am filled to overflowing with His love. He is an awesome God, and He is my life. I am no longer fearful because He promises that nothing can ever separate me from His love.

> And I am convinced that nothing can ever separate us from His love. Death can't, and life can't. The angels can't, and the demons can't. Our fears for today, our worries about tomorrow, and even the powers of hell can't keep God's love away. Whether we are high above the sky or in the deepest ocean, nothing in all creation will ever be able to separate us from the love of God that is revealed in Christ Jesus our Lord.
>
> Romans 8:38–39 (NLT)

Just in case we don't come back—the seven words that became a harsh reality and forever changed my life that summer. I now know that in my times of darkness and loneliness, God was there the entire time. He cried when I cried, and He hurt when I hurt. All of my hardships were experiences that God would later use me for to comfort others in their time of need. 2 Corinthians 1:3-4 (NASB) says, "Blessed be the God and Father of our Lord Jesus Christ, the Father of mercies and God of all comfort, who comforts us in all our affliction, so that we may be able to comfort those who are in any affliction, with the comfort with which we ourselves are comforted by God."

God is so faithful to me, even when I am not faithful to Him (2 Timothy 2:13). As one of His daughters, I'm not perfect—just forgiven—forgiven for everything in the past, present, and future. "If we confess our sins, He is faithful and righteous to forgive us our sins and to cleanse us from all unrighteousness" (1 John 1:9, NASB).

This year, Bob and I celebrated twenty-five years of marriage, and I have a great relationship with all of my family. I love the verse from Jeremiah 29:11 (NIV): "'For I know the plans I have for you,' declares the Lord, 'plans to prosper you and not to harm you, plans to give you hope and a future.'" I dedicate this verse to my daughters, Kayla and Jenna, as they continue their journey with Jesus. Praying for them and with them has been a pleasure and an honor as a mother.

P.S. I miss my sister.

Note from Lori

My little sister Ellen was dealing with secrets of her own. She hid things about herself so that no one would know the truth about her. She tried to look good on the outside but was miserable on the inside. Just three short months after Shelly was saved, Ellen finally came to the end of her secrets and the end of herself. She was desperate for answers.

Battle of the Mind: Ellen's Story

If your sinful nature controls your mind, there is death. But if the Holy Spirit controls your mind, there is life and peace.

Romans 8:6 (NLT)

It was my last day of middle school. My friend and I decided to celebrate a little early. We sat on her bed and giggled as we ate donuts and drank orange juice and vodka. As we hurried out the door, we quickly hid the bottles underneath her bed and walked to school. By the time we got there, we were pretty tipsy. We told everyone what we had done, and they thought it was pretty cool. Later that day, we found out that my friend's older sister had discovered the bottles under the bed and told their dad. When he confronted us, we told him we would never do it again, and I pleaded with him not to tell my parents. He never did, and my secret was safe.

I never did keep my promise to him, but instead continued drinking throughout my high school years. To tell you the truth, I never really gave it much thought because everyone else drank, and it just seemed like the thing to do.

At the end of my senior year and just seventeen years old, I moved out of my parents' home and into an apartment with my older sister, Barb. When she asked me to move in with her, I was really excited. I thought she asked because she liked me, but I found out later it was because she couldn't afford to live on her own and needed the other half of the rent. Nonetheless, I was so excited to be on my own. I got my first job and bought a car. As much as I liked my car, I asked Barb if she would trade from time to time because I really liked hers. She would always selfishly say no.

One hot, summer day, out of the blue, she said she was willing to trade cars for the entire summer! "Are you serious?" I asked. We exchanged keys, and I couldn't wait to drive to work the next day. When I went to turn on the air conditioner, I realized her car didn't even have one. *You have got to be kidding!* When I got home, I told her I wanted my car back. She said that I had agreed to keep it for the summer, and that was that. I couldn't believe it! And this was only one of many surprises I had coming. I entered the bar scene as a young teen. The local bars had what was called Teen Nights, a mock version of the bar scene without the alcohol. They had bouncers at the door, and it was a night of dancing and drinking sodas. I found out that the bouncers at Teen Nights were the same ones who were at the real nightclubs. I became friends with all of them and got a fake ID so I could get in. I began to drink almost every night of the week. Partying was my life. I was foul-mouthed and very opinionated, and I was known as the queen of dirty jokes.

Within six months of moving into our apartment, Barb left and moved in with her boyfriend, Denny. Two more roommates came and went, and because I couldn't afford to live there by myself, I decided to find a new place to live. I found a sweet little basement apartment in the home of an older married couple. This would be perfect. Now I would be totally on my own and not have to answer to anyone.

I was at a college party one night and met a girl who would become my next best friend. She introduced me to a whole new set of friends, partying, and games. One of those was a drinking game we played in the car. If we got stopped at a red light, we would see how many times we could swig the alcohol from the bottle before the light turned green. *One...two... three...four...five...six...*

One morning, after a night out on the town, I woke up in my bed still wearing my winter coat. I didn't know how I got there, and it really scared me. I frantically looked at the clock. Nine thirty a.m.! *Oh no! I'm supposed to be at work!* The last thing I remembered was being at a night club with my friend and her boyfriend. I called her to see what had happened. She began laughing as she told me how they had to carry me to the car and then into my apartment because I had passed out at the bar. After work that day, I went out again. I guess it didn't scare me enough.

My best friend and I were out one night when I was introduced to a guy named Jim. He loved partying almost as much as I did. We hit it off right away and began dating. I now had another drinking partner. *Life just got better.* We loved being together and went to the movies and out to eat a lot. No matter where we went, our beer went with us; yes, even to the movie theaters.

We dated for about three years before we got married. I had it all: a husband I loved, a great job, money, and a new home. The only thing missing was the white picket fence, and if I would have asked for it, I would have gotten it. I was very controlling and selfish, not to mention independent. I was my own boss, and no one was going to tell me what to do.

Several years into our marriage, we had a son named Austin. It wasn't until we had him that we both realized that we could not have made this beautiful little boy on our own. We decided to attend church the next week because we thought it was the right thing to do. We loved all the attention we got as we walked in the doors with our new little baby. Week after week we continued to go but for all the wrong reasons. We had cut back on our drinking because we were parents now and figured we were supposed to be a little more responsible. Right?

About a year and a half later, I got pregnant again. In my eighteenth week of pregnancy, I woke up in a pool of blood, and my husband and I rushed to the hospital. They told me I had a complication of pregnancy called a bleeding placenta previa. They dismissed us from the hospital and told us to see my doctor as soon as possible. The next morning, we went to see him. After he examined me, he sent us back to the hospital. We had no idea that he was sending me back there because he thought I was having a miscarriage. We checked into the hospital, and they informed me that I was going to be bedridden. For the next fifteen weeks, I was flat on my back. I was determined to be strong, but I had no faith, no hope, and no idea how I was going to get through this. I wasn't going to let anybody know that I was starting to fall apart.

When I was around six months pregnant, the doctor told me that I was going to have to stay in the hospital until I delivered. After being in the hospital for a couple of weeks, I had had enough. I needed to talk to someone I could trust, so I called my sister, Lori. I was crying and told her I couldn't handle it anymore. I wanted her to get mad with me and tell me how bad she felt for me, but instead she asked if she could pray. It sounded kind of weird, but I was desperate and told her that would be fine. As soon as she started praying on the phone, I felt this peace come over me and cover me like a blanket. It felt like a huge burden had been lifted. No one had ever asked if they could pray for me. I thanked her, and before I could hang up, the nurse came in and said I could go home on a monitor.

I continued to follow my doctor's orders down to the last detail. I had about three and a half weeks left. I was in bed one morning on the home monitor, and I suddenly realized I was lying in another pool of blood. I ended up back in the hospital and was bleeding all through the night. The doctor came in and checked me and said he would see me next week if I made it that long. He left to go to another hospital for more rounds. I asked the nurse how long they expected this to continue. She said, "As long as you can keep that baby in there!"

After she left, I looked up at the ceiling and desperately cried out loud, "I can't do this anymore!"

Right then, the nurse came running in. I thought she had heard me because I said it so loud. She was so excited and said, "You won't believe this! The doctor just called and said he's turning around and coming back to the hospital. Get ready! We are going to deliver the baby right now!"

We had a healthy baby boy. Ryan was born on May 20, 1993 and weighed seven pounds and eight ounces.

Looking back, I thought the events that led up to Ryan's birth were mere coincidences: the home monitoring, the doctor coming back to the hospital, etc,... but now I realize that God was in control of my life even back then.

We now had two sons, and our life continued on. One beautiful summer day, my dad stopped by to see Ryan. We were all sitting outside in lawn chairs when a car pulled up in my driveway. It was my sister, Barb. *Whoa! What's she doing here?* We hadn't spoken in almost three years. She lived seventy-five miles away, so it wasn't like she was just in the neighborhood. I could hardly remember what had caused the three-year silence, but I knew that neither of us was willing to give in.

She was smiling as she walked up the driveway. "What are you doing here?" I nervously asked her.

She just matter-of-factly answered, "I just came to see you."

We both stood there smiling at each other. I was in shock, to say the least, but I was so happy to see her. With an awkward silence between us, I quickly asked, "Do you want to go in the house and see Austin?"

"Sure!" she answered. I can't explain what happened next, but it was as if the three years of silence had never existed. The cold looks, the harsh words, the hatred, and the broken relationship we had experienced was gone. I couldn't put my finger on it, but there was something different about Barb. There was a softness I had never seen before, not to mention the fact that she was even speaking to me.

A couple of days later, Barb called and asked me to forgive her for everything that had happened. *Wow! Something had really changed. This is not the Barb I had known at all.* I had never heard her ask for forgiveness for anything. I told her I was sorry too, and our relationship was completely restored.

Even though Jim and I appeared to have it all together on the outside, we were dead on the inside. I knew I was missing something, so I began my search to find what would make me happy. I started going on shopping sprees for clothes. I had every style and type of clothing you could imagine: winter, spring, summer, fall, fun clothes, weekend clothes, night clothes, and sports clothes. I had titles for it all. After that failed to satisfy me, I moved on to chocolate binges. Before work, I would go to the convenience store and buy candy bars, tootsie rolls, and anything chocolate. One time, I was so embarrassed I told a clerk at a convenience store that the mound of chocolate I was purchasing was for my kids. She said, "Wow, aren't you a nice mommy!"

I was so tired of hiding and I was miserable. I continued to seek things that would satisfy my need for the "perfect life" but never found it. The only thing I did find was that I was sinking deeper and deeper into depression and had no way to escape the darkness. Deep down, I didn't want anyone to know that I didn't have it all—that I wasn't perfect. My husband and kids seemed fine, so maybe I just needed to lighten up. I continued telling myself there wasn't anything wrong. The truth was, I had never felt so frightened and all alone before.

I saw a commercial on TV about some pills that could help with PMS and/or depression. *This is it. This might help me!* I set up an appointment to see my doctor. I didn't think he would give me the pills if I told him I was depressed, so I lied and told him that I was having trouble with PMS. On top of that, I didn't really want him to know either. He gave me a prescription, and I was so excited to finally get help for my sadness. I felt hopeful, but my hope was short-lived. The medicine didn't even touch the heavy despair that I was feeling.

One night, as my husband and I were lying in bed, I began sobbing uncontrollably. My body began to shake. He had never seen me like this and had no idea that anything was wrong, because I had even fooled him. He was as scared as I was and began crying with me.

"What should we do?" he asked.

"I don't know," I said. I started thinking about the peace I felt when Lori had prayed for me in the hospital and I wanted that calm and peaceful feeling again. I told him I needed to talk to Lori, so I called her as soon as I got up the next morning.

I explained to her some of what was going on, but I didn't tell her that I had been taking medication every day for my depression. I told her that I wanted to go to one of those retreats that Barb had gone to. I knew if it could change Barb, then it could change anyone. She said she would call around to see if there was one coming up.

She called me back in about five minutes. "There is one in a couple of weeks," she said. "Can you go?" I immediately said yes and started making arrangements.

When I got on the plane, I had no clue where I was going, what a retreat was, or why I had even asked to go to one, but I was determined to make a fresh start and leave everything behind, even my medication. I had exhausted every avenue I could think of to make me feel better, and this was my last hope.

As we pulled up to the retreat campus, I saw a statue of a woman holding a cup, standing by a well. I asked Lori about it, and she told me it was probably the theme for the weekend. I had no idea who this woman was or why she would be standing at a well, and I certainly had no idea what was about to take place in my life. I remember standing in the registration line just watching everyone and thinking that I had never been surrounded by so many women before. Everyone seemed so nice and genuine.

When I reached the inside of the doorway, one of the ladies who was greeting everyone hugged me tight and said, "I'm so glad you're here!"

I turned around to Lori and said, "I think she really wants me to be here!" I will never forget that hug as long as I live.

Friday night was fun. This was all so new to me and I was trying to take it all in. I couldn't imagine what we would be doing all weekend and how they would fill up our time. It was fun spending time with Lori and her friends, Vanessa and Lisa, but I wasn't feeling too connected at this point. I was definitely out of my comfort zone.

The next day, I was looking ahead on the schedule preparing myself for anything that might be uncomfortable. There was an hour blocked off for "quiet time" later that day. When I read the words *quiet* and *hour*, it seemed like an eternity. I started feeling a little anxious about it because I didn't know what it meant. I asked Lori what we were supposed to do during that hour. She said it was a time when you were just supposed to be alone, think about your life and where you are at with God. *Oh no. I don't want to be alone. I don't want to be quiet for an hour.*

The time came to dismiss for quiet time. I followed everyone outside and I walked around until I found a spot by a beautiful palm tree overlooking a pond with ducks in it. I decided to just sit and watch the ducks the whole time and wait until the hour was up. I looked around at all the women. Some were in groups of two, sitting quietly together, but most of them were by themselves. *What are they thinking? What are they reading?* I took out the folder they had given us, and on it were some questions and scriptures. I had never read the Bible before, so I just sat there for a while, not knowing what to do. I then got out some paper and started to write down my thoughts.

I am not sure how to pray for things in my life. Is what I'm experiencing the same as everyone else? I don't feel out of place here, but there are times when I hear everyone talking about verses in the Bible, and I begin to feel unsettled. I'm so unsure of what is happening in my life right now. I was giving up mentally and physically. I don't know why I'm struggling so hard. Nothing is helping, and I can't believe I'm here. It has been overwhelming from the minute I walked in.

By the time I was done writing, the tears started flowing. They weren't tears of sadness, they were tears of joy. The hour was over before I knew it, and the women were all starting to move around and talk again.

It was time for the Saturday night session. The music was playing and everyone was singing. I didn't know any of the words or the melodies of the music, so I just read along. The words started jumping off the page and really struck a chord in my heart. I especially remember the words, "Lord, I need an undivided heart..."

That was exactly what I wanted...an *undivided heart*. I started getting nervous, and this warm sensation came over me. I felt like I wanted to run out of there, but I didn't know where I would run or what I was running from. Besides, I began to envision how silly it would look if I ran. Right then, Lori put her arm around me, and it felt as though she was holding me down. I tried to hide my emotions and hold everything back, but I felt like I was going to burst.

As the worship time came to an end, the speaker began the next session. My heart calmed down, and I was able to give her my full attention. As she began teaching, she explained the significance of the woman at the well. Jesus told the woman, "Everyone who drinks of this water will thirst again; but whoever drinks of the water that I will give him shall never thirst; but the water that I will give him will become in him a well of water springing up to eternal life" (John 4:13-14, NASB).

That was me! I had been drinking from the water of my own well instead of the water that Jesus gives, and it had left me thirsty. I tried to take it all in, but my mind was spinning. I had a lot to think about when I went to bed that night.

After the session on Sunday morning, I was thinking about what I had heard, about how Jesus was beaten and crucified and took the punishment for my sins so that I could be accepted by God. Those words penetrated my heart.

> But He was wounded and crushed for our sins. He was beaten that we might have peace. He was whipped, and we were healed! All of us have strayed away like sheep. We have left God's paths to follow our own. Yet the Lord laid on Him the guilt and sins of us all.
>
> Isaiah 53:5–6 (NLT)

The retreat came to a close, and we went back to our rooms to pack. I looked at Lori and said, "I've never known what Jesus's death was about!" I was so excited about what I had heard. I didn't understand it completely at the time, but the Lord opened my heart to hear and understand the gospel message. Before we could finish our conversation, Vanessa and Lisa came in, and we all sat down on the beds. My heart was racing.

As we started talking, Lisa looked at me and asked if I wanted to pray to repent and receive Jesus. I didn't hesitate to say yes! We all bowed our heads and prayed. Tears began flowing down my face as I asked Jesus to forgive me of my sins and be the Lord and Savior of my life. Within seconds, everyone was crying. We all hugged afterward, and everyone was really excited.

Left to Right—Lisa, Vanessa, Lori, and me

On the way home, we stopped at a gas station. I looked at the clerk behind the counter. *I wonder if he knows Jesus.* That was the first time that I had ever thought about that before, and I have not stopped asking that question to this day about everyone I see!

I could not wait to tell my husband, Jim, what had happened, even though I didn't fully understand it myself. When I walked off the plane, it felt like I walked into a whole new world. I couldn't quit smiling, and this time it was real.

As I settled back into my life, I couldn't help wondering if the peace and joy I felt would last. I was fearful that it would be temporary, like everything else in my life. I'm sure my husband was wondering the same thing as he began watching this new me. He was curious as to why I was so peaceful, why I stopped drinking and didn't need my medication anymore, and why my foul mouth was gone. He started doing some research on his own. I would see him reading the Bible at night, but we never talked about it. The Bible was not anything we had ever discussed before, so it was hard to carry on a conversation about it.

About a year later, Jim went to a Christian conference for men. I couldn't wait to talk to him when he got home. When he returned, I sat there listening, and I could already see a change in him. He said he was sitting in the stadium alone after everyone had gone on a lunch break. They had been talking about loving God and obeying Him, and he realized that he couldn't love someone he didn't know, much less obey Him. He had always lived his life independent of God, never realizing that he was a sinner or thinking about what Jesus had gone through on his behalf. He said he looked up to the sky and cried out to the Lord and told Him that he was afraid and tired of trying to do everything on his own. He wanted to be the husband and father he should be to me and our boys, but he needed help. He asked God for forgiveness, and right there sitting on the bleachers, he surrendered everything. He asked Jesus to take control and be the Lord and Savior of his life. Jim met his Savior that day just like I met Him at the retreat.

Shortly after Jim got saved, we were lying in bed one night and prayed together for the first time. We dedicated our marriage and our two sons to the Lord. By God's grace, we just celebrated our twenty-fourth wedding anniversary!

I was striving for perfection my whole life, and I failed at every turn. Why? Because I never have been nor ever will be perfect. The only difference now is that I *know* the One who is perfect, and I have put my faith and trust in Him.

To win the battle of my mind, I have to constantly renew it each day with the Word of God. It has been the source of my hope and joy since I surrendered my life to Him fifteen years ago. The hug at the door, the quiet time, the music, and finally my sin exposed—it was all pointing to the reality of what I was missing: a relationship with Jesus Christ.

The only thing I thirst for now is more of Him.

Note from Lori

Now there were four of us with completely new hearts and lives. It was so amazing to watch God as He drew each of us to Himself one by one. We kept praying for the rest of the family. It had only been a year since Ellen's transformation when we invited the last two— my sister Kerry and my sister-in-law Donna, to go on a retreat with us. We were so excited when they both said they could go! Kerry had professed to being a Christian for about eight years, but I knew that she had not surrendered her life and acknowledged Jesus as her Lord and Savior. Like the rest of us, she thought she was okay with God as long as she was a pretty good person. God was about to open her eyes to the truth...

From Victim to Victory: Kerry's Story

The Lord is my strength and my song; He has become my victory.

Exodus 15:2 (NLT)

Imagine a small town where everybody knew each other, a place where it was safe to leave your door unlocked during the night, without the fear of someone breaking in. Imagine a place where it was safe for children to walk the neighborhood streets to school and friends' houses without the typical parental concern for the child's safety and well-being. Welcome to Dixon, Nebraska, home to approximately one hundred people, and home to the Kuhl family—my family! To the outside world, the small town of Dixon was a "cookie-cutter" ideal of the charming, friendly, and cozy town.

When I say that Dixon was home to the Kuhl family, I was not simply referring to my parents and siblings. Just up the hill from our home lived my grandparents and Aunt Deb, and a couple of blocks away from them lived my uncle Lynn, aunt Anita, and my two cousins. Needless to say, we were a very close-knit family who did almost everything together. Every Sunday after church, we would all gather at my grandparents' home for breakfast. I can still almost smell the freshly baked cinnamon rolls coming out of the oven. My days were spent playing hide-and-seek, climbing the cherry trees in the backyard, or playing dolls in the attic. I lived a pretty charmed life in my safe and secure little town. However, the characteristics of *safe* and *secure* weren't words that I would use to describe Dixon for long—at least not for me.

Whenever Mom and Dad went out together, they hired a trusted neighbor boy in his teens to babysit. We all liked him a lot in the beginning. Who wouldn't love a babysitter who would play games with you instead of talking on the phone or watching television all night? But as time went on, his games were not fun anymore. He would make my brother and I help him scare the little ones, Lori and Barb, who were only two and three at the time, by telling scary stories in the dark. I even remember one time he put ketchup all over my brother, then laid a knife next to him, and told all of us that Dave had gotten stabbed and was dead.

From there, it just got worse. When it was time to go to bed, he made everyone go—except me. I thought I was pretty cool to be able to stay up late—until I found out why.

Me and my little brother Dave

I was only about six years old when he started sexually molesting me. He continually threatened me, saying that if I told anyone, he could make the games that we played become a reality. He would remind me over and over again that my mom and dad would be "really mad" at me if I told them what happened. He said, if anything *did* happen to my brothers and sisters, they would blame me. So I kept quiet. I was so ashamed of what had happened, but more than that, I was fearful of what he might do to my brothers and sisters or me if I told anyone.

I *never* told my parents, or anyone else for that matter, but you can only imagine the relief that I felt when my family moved from Dixon to a new city when I was eight years old. I felt safe away from him and safe with my secret. I buried the truth about what happened and believed that it was my fault.

As an eight-year-old, I knew that God existed somewhere up in heaven, but to me He was unapproachable—a God who was not personal at all and who had lots of rules to follow. I thought God was like Santa Claus—He could see everything I did, and I better be good or I wouldn't go to heaven. Because of that, and because of my secret, I wanted to be anyone *but* me, because being *me* wasn't good enough.

Even though moving away was a relief and somewhat exciting, starting third grade at a new school was very scary. I went from having two other classmates in Dixon to having almost thirty! I remember walking into the classroom the first day and being so intimidated by the number of kids that were there.

It didn't take long before I began making friends, and within a short time, my new best friend Kathy and I were inseparable. We loved going to the movies, to the skating rink, and to each other's houses to hang out. My parents didn't always allow me to do the things that everyone else was doing, so at an early age, I began to rebel. In junior high, I was so excited when I made the cheerleading squad. I gained instant popularity with the status of "cheerleader," and I felt as though I really belonged.

When it came time to attend high school, my parents allowed me to choose where I would go. I chose a small private high school, mainly because I knew it would be easier to be accepted there. Still not allowed to do all the things that my friends were doing, I continued to push the limits of my parents' rules. Desperately trying to keep up my image, my rebellion continued to be the source of conflict in our relationship.

The school I attended had very strict rules. The teachers were very controlling and legalistic. They weren't even nice to the "good" kids, so it became the cool thing to rebel. The more defiant you were, the more popular you became with the kids. So I rebelled with the best of them, and at my little school I gained acceptance and approval from my peers, and it felt good.

During my sophomore year, a guy from the public school called and asked me out. I didn't know Mick at the time, but I knew *of* him. I felt like he was definitely out of my league because he was extremely popular and could date anyone he wanted—so why me? I immediately thought it must be a bet, but he turned out to be sincere and a really nice guy. He was my very first date and the first guy I ever felt like I could be myself around. We dated throughout the summer, but we broke up when a college guy stole my attention. JR was a rebel, and he always said he was going to change the world, but I'm pretty sure that the only world he changed was mine. He introduced me to alcohol and drugs, and my life became a downhill spiral. My parents saw drastic changes in me and decided to put me in counseling. I was so good at lying by this time, I was even able to con the counselors.

My parents decided to transfer me to a different private school for my senior year of high school. I was devastated. My feelings of acceptance from so many of my peers dwindled down to nothing. I went from a school of eighty students to a school of eight hundred. No one knew me, and no one cared. JR convinced me that he was the only one who really cared about me and understood what I was going through, so I became totally dependent on him for my worth and acceptance. This came at a high price. He continually told me about all the college girls that he could be with, so he wanted me to prove to him how much I loved him. He said he needed to know how important he was to me or he would move on. I thought I would eventually have to have sex with him, and I was scared. I knew in my heart it was wrong, but he was my only world at this point, and I didn't want to lose him.

While JR was home on Christmas break, I finally gave in to him. I didn't think it could happen on the first time, but I soon found out I was pregnant. I was only seventeen years old. My first thoughts were not about my parents or even me. I was obsessed with him. *Well, this is forever now. He will always be with me, and we will get married and live happily ever after like my parents.* Then I began to doubt everything. *Will he marry me? Does he love me? He said he did…or did he?*

As you can probably guess, he was *not* happy when he found out about the pregnancy. He took off for a month to *find himself.* My parents were more than devastated when they found out. They didn't like the way he treated me, and they didn't like what I had become since dating him. They begged me not to marry him and offered to do anything to help. I was determined to prove to them that he loved me and that he would never leave me. I knew the only way to make everything right was to get him to marry me.

After JR got back from *finding himself,* we got into a huge fight. He yelled and screamed and ended up hitting me. He apologized and said he would never do it again. He said he did it because he felt trapped and that I just needed to understand that. I accepted his reasons for hitting me because he had convinced me that it was my fault, so I told no one. Actually, he convinced me that *all* of his problems were because of me, and that I was lucky that he would stay with me. I believed him. His parents told him that he needed to do the right thing and marry me, so a few months later we were married.

We moved into a small, run-down apartment about fifteen miles from my hometown. I remember he was always angry about anything and everything. He would yell, and I would cower. I did everything he told me to just to please him and not make any waves, but nothing was ever good enough. I was scared all the time and lived in fear of his temper and mean, critical remarks and outbursts.

Within one month of being married, he began hitting me in his angry rages. I endured black eyes, fat lips, cuts, bruises, and broken ribs. He would often threaten to leave me and then take off for a while. He would come back, apologize, and say he would never do it again. He always blamed his outbursts on something *I* did, and I would end up apologizing, all the while thinking, *Maybe this time he will change.*

My life was a mess, and I was living a nightmare. I was married to an abusive alcohol and drug addict, and I lived in total fear. I continued to make excuses for visible evidences of the beatings, because I didn't want to bring more shame on myself. Not only that, I was so afraid of what he would do if I ever told someone the truth. I felt like I was in too deep at this point and had nowhere to go. Besides, I believed this was my punishment for getting pregnant, and I would just have to live with it. Whenever we would get into an argument, he told me not to even think about leaving him because I would be a worthless, used-up, divorced woman with a kid who no one would want. I believed the lies he told me. I knew that whatever it took, I had to make this marriage work because I was stuck for "better or for worse." I thought maybe if I would be a better wife, he would not get worse, but he did get worse—much worse. The beatings became more frequent and much more severe.

When my son Jeremy was almost a year old, I began to experience severe attacks of pain. I was bedridden off and on for over a year. I was in three different hospitals with three different diagnoses until they finally discovered it was a non-functioning gall bladder and bleeding ulcers due to stress. The pains were worse than childbirth, and I was left with a one-year-old to care for. I wasn't about to ask for help, because if I did, everyone would know that JR was out partying all the time. He would often come home and tell me about his countless affairs, but I never said a word. I couldn't deal with all the physical pain of the attacks *and* the beatings at the same time, so I said nothing.

One night, he flew into a rage and started throwing things at me off the kitchen counters. Then, one by one, he emptied out every cupboard, throwing everything at the walls, at the floor, and then at me. He began tossing everything from the refrigerator and moved onto the furniture. When he had thrown and broken everything in sight, he started on me. He began punching and kicking me, and throwing me around. As I laid there shielding myself, I saw Jeremy, who was not quite two, watching from the other side of the room. He was crying hysterically. "Please don't hit me in front of Jeremy!" I begged him. He drug me by my hair outside and proceeded to kick and punch me over and over again until I couldn't move. By the time he was done, I was beaten both physically *and* emotionally. He told me he was going to the bar, and when he got back, he wanted everything cleaned up and his bags packed. My only thought was, *How am I going to get all that done before he comes back?* I was so afraid he was going to kill me if I didn't.

His brother stopped by, and this time there was no way I could hide this beating. The house was a mess, and I was a mess. He raced off to get his parents, and when they saw me, they immediately called my mom and dad. That night, I ended up at the hospital with guards at my door. I was thankful to be safe and actually relieved that my parents knew. I ended up having gallbladder surgery and recuperating at their home. I felt so ashamed and worthless.

The whole time I was recuperating, I kept thinking about how angry he was going to be now that everyone knew our secret. I was so afraid of the day when I would have to go home, but before I was completely healed, JR had an accident at work. He had fallen eighty feet from the scaffolding at his construction job, suffering severe head and internal injuries. He was in a coma, and the doctors didn't think he had much of a chance to live. Even though my first thought was that God was punishing him for all the times he had beaten me, I knew I needed to be there with him. I immediately went to the hospital. I stayed night and day with him for about six weeks until he regained consciousness and was eventually released. The trauma to his brain caused him to lose speech and motor skills and his ability to speak well, so he was very dependent on me to take him back and forth to therapy. It was a full-time job taking care of him, but I thought maybe this was a chance for a new start. He was quite mellow at first, but once he was back to driving again, he was pretty much back to all his old behaviors of hanging out and partying at the bars with other girls.

I got a call one night from Mick, my "first date nice guy." He asked me why my husband was in a bar acting as though he wasn't married. For the first time, I poured my heart out to him like I had never done with anyone else before. I told him the reason I stayed was because I didn't believe in divorce, and I didn't want to be alone. "And besides," I said to him, "who would want a divorced woman with a kid?" Mick was so sweet. He said he knew a lot of guys that would marry me, and he was one of them. I believe he gave me the encouragement that I needed to leave JR if he beat me again. Before we hung up, he said, "If it works out for you, great, but if he beats you again and you don't leave, I won't feel sorry for you." Those words stayed with me.

Not long after, on a Sunday afternoon, we were heading to a baseball game. As we were driving, JR confronted me about telling his parents about the beating the night I went to the hospital. He became enraged and began punching me. My little boy, Jeremy, was in the middle of us in the front seat. JR picked him up and threw him against the back window to get at me. I begged him to stop. He slammed the car into park and pushed me out. He got out and kept punching and kicking me. People were passing by, but when they saw the rage in him, they kept driving. He went back to the car, threw Jeremy out, and took off. I remember running the twelve blocks to my parents' house. I was hysterical, and what was worse, Jeremy was hysterical. We stayed with my parents for about a month until I could rent a little apartment close by.

The next six months were awful. He would follow me, harass me, and try to manipulate and guilt me into coming back, but I stood strong because of Jeremy. I figured that *I* might deserve the beatings, but I wouldn't allow my little boy to ever have to go through that again. I had come to the realization that I didn't want that kind of life for myself *or* my son. I never went back.

One night, while Jeremy was sleeping, JR broke in and started beating me. When he started choking me, I thought he was going to kill me, and he might have if my brother hadn't shown up. Dave threatened to kill him if he ever touched me again. After that night, I decided that I needed to move as far away as possible. Looking back, it was only by God's grace that I made it out of that relationship alive.

At twenty years of age, and with my two-year-old, I packed up and headed for California where my grandparents lived. Before I left, Mick and I rekindled our friendship. He was my true loyal friend, my encourager, my protector, and what seemed to be my "knight in shining armor." He eventually ended up in California, and we moved in together. Even though I knew it was wrong, I justified living with him because of what happened before. There was no way I would ever consider marrying someone without living with them first. Not only that, but I had blown my first chance with him, and I wasn't going to lose him a second time. Mick also had his own unresolved issues from the past and neither of us had a real purpose for our lives.

After two years of living together, we got married. Because of what I had gone through, I decided that I wasn't *ever* going to let anyone control me again. I was going to be totally and completely happy this time because *I* was in control.

When it came time to put Jeremy in first grade, we enrolled him in private school. I knew this was something my parents would want, and I wanted to make them proud because of everything I had put them through. I also went back to church, attending every week, thinking not only would this make my parents happy, but it just might fill the void in my life and make me happy also. But the more I went, the more it became a duty. I thought that if I didn't go, and if I didn't obey the rules, something bad would happen, so I kept going.

In 1979, our second son, Jobey, was born. Mick also graduated from college and landed a promising career with a highly reputable advertising illustration firm in Los Angeles. *Well,* I thought, *this would be the answer to what I was missing—money!* I thought we would be happier now because we would be making a lot of money, and I felt like we were on our way to fulfilling all of our dreams.

We moved to a new home in the hills above Burbank, California, and my new neighbor was exactly who I wanted to be. Nanette was beautiful, worked for CBS, knew lots of movie stars, and her husband seemed to adore her. *If only I could be like her.* She had a daughter, and oh, how I wanted a daughter. Shortly after, I became pregnant, and nine months later we welcomed our daughter, Kacey, into the world. My life seemed perfect. Nanette and I became best friends, and we did everything together. She was all about glitz and glamour and material things like I'd never seen before. I watched her husband lavish her with jewels and furs, which to me became symbolic of how much he loved her. I wanted Mick to be like that; thus, my expectations of him began.

My days were filled with going to the gym, going to breakfast, shopping, out for lunch, going shopping again, and then partying on the weekends. Keeping up with my image and striving to be like her wasn't easy, but it was fun. I put my friendship with her far above everything else, including my marriage. The more I became like her, the more my relationship with Mick suffered. He got sick of me trying to be someone else, and even more sick of me wanting *him* to be someone else. We continued to party and go on trips with them. They moved to a bigger and better house, so we moved to a bigger and better house. Mick worked night and day to keep up with the Joneses thinking that the more he gave me the happier I would be. Not so. It was never enough.

By this time, Jeremy was fourteen years old and very much out of control. I felt so much guilt from the past and always blamed his problems on that. The truth was that he was becoming just like me. He lied, cheated, stole, and was in trouble at school all the time. His sporadic behavior was more than we could handle, and I was at my end with him. All of this was really taking a toll on our marriage, and I cried over and over to Lori about him. She sat me down and told me I needed to admit I couldn't do it anymore without God's help. She explained how I needed to give up control and give him to the Lord. I was so ready to give him to *anyone* who would help, so she prayed with me, and I felt so relieved. I thought I was really right with God now, but what I didn't realize at the time is that I was willing to give him Jeremy's life over and over, but I wasn't willing to give him my own.

Mick continued to strive more and more to make us all happy with material things. He began fighting bouts of depression from working so much. He was tired of trying to keep up with the spending. One day, he decided we should move back to the Midwest where the cost of living was lower. I wasn't at all excited about it, but I thought maybe if he didn't have to work so hard, he would be happier and then I would be too. So, off we went to a dream come true for Mick—a beautiful home on a golf course. Now I had to figure out how I was going to fit in to a society of country clubbers. My life again revolved around finding acceptance by drinking and being the life of the weekend parties. Mick and I continued to fight a lot. There were so many times I would pack my bags to leave and go back to California. We went to counselors and psychiatrists and nothing seemed to work.

Even though I thought going to church every Sunday was enough, Lori kept telling me to find a Bible study. I finally decided to have one at my house, but I continued to party on the weekends with that same group of girls. (Does that sound like someone else in my family? At least I wasn't leading it).

After three more years of being what I thought everybody else wanted me to be, I could no longer keep up. I was exhausted. I had come to the end of myself— whoever *that* was. I didn't have the strength to fight the battle within me. I blamed other people and my circumstances for my unhappiness. Jeremy was drinking and doing drugs and living with his pregnant girl-friend. Jobey was suffering with depression and occasional thoughts of suicide and was in weekly counseling and on anti-depressants. My daughter, Kacey, was striving for popularity just like I had done. Our home was in chaos, and I was scared and depressed. For two weeks, I could barely get out of bed.

I called Lori *again,* told her I was at my end *again,* and that I was coming out to visit. When I went to California, she talked to me for two to three days about Jesus and the real purpose for my life and my marriage. She told me I needed to take my focus off of Mick to fulfill all my needs and focus on Jesus. She gave me teaching tapes on Philippians about how to have joy in all circumstances. I came home with a new hopeful feeling. I saturated myself for five months with those tapes until October of 1996, when I was to go to a retreat with all of my sisters. Retreats, up until that point for me, were pretty much a fun, girl time get-together that always made me feel better because I felt accepted by friends, family, and God. This retreat would be fun because the six of us would all be together. Plus, this one seemed non-threatening. The theme was from Joshua 24:15, "Choose for your-selves today whom you will serve…" *This will be easy. I serve God. I go to church. I have my kids in private school. I'm doing it right,* I thought.

On Friday night, a bunch of us got together in one of the rooms to hang out. One after the other, they began talking about their relationship with Jesus and how they got saved. I was very uneasy and anxious, maybe even defensive. The next night, I was more at ease, but my stomach was in knots. As I listened intently to the speaker, she asked the question, "What is it that is keeping you from being everything Jesus wants you to be?" I had always thought, for the most part anyway, that I was everything I was *supposed* to be. I had no idea how far I had missed the mark, but God was about to show me. I knew I didn't have the joy and excitement for the Lord that my sisters had, and I wondered why. As I crawled into bed that night, I desperately begged God to show me if there was anything holding me back. I really wanted to know.

Sunday morning came, and the speaker began sharing her testimony. *Her story could be my story!* I had never heard anyone speak so freely and with such transparency. I listened closely to every word she spoke. I was mesmerized. It was as if my life was flashing before me. As the speaker continued sharing the details of her life, God began to reveal to me the details of mine. He showed me that I was not responsible for what had happened to me all those years ago, but I *was* responsible for the way I responded to those hurts. God also showed me that I needed to quit hiding and let go of the shame, guilt, and fear that I had carried for so long. I don't remember exactly what she said at the end, but her words convicted me to the core. I had focused on everyone else's sin and what had been done to me. But God opened my eyes to see that the things I had called my "problems" were really sins against a Holy God. I realized for the first time that I had been hiding not only my secret but also my sin.

> When I refused to confess my sin, I was weak and miserable, and I groaned all day long. Finally, I confessed all my sins to You and stopped trying to hide them. I said to myself, "I will confess my rebellion to the Lord." And You forgave me! All my guilt is gone.
>
> Psalm 32:3–5 (NLT)

As the speaker finished telling her story, she shared the gospel message with us. She said we were sinners in need of a Savior, and that we desperately needed to be reconciled to God. I was broken and excited at the same time. I raised my hand in total surrender to Jesus, repented of my sins, and confessed Him as Lord and Savior.

> If you confess with your mouth that Jesus is Lord and believe in your heart that God raised Him from the dead, you will be saved. For it is by believing in your heart that you are made right with God, and it is by confessing with your mouth that you are saved.
>
> Romans 10:9–10 (NLT)

The weight of my sin was gone, and I was overwhelmed with joy. For the first time in my life, I was able to understand the things of God. I was finally set free from the bondage of living life for me. "...and He died for all, so that they who live might no longer live for themselves, but for Him who died and rose again on their behalf" (2 Corinthians 5:15, NASB). The only ruler of my life now is Jesus Christ. My love and obedience toward Him is no longer out of fear but out of an appreciation for what He has done for me, and it is only possible because His spirit now lives in me. "And

I will put My Spirit in you so you will obey My laws and do whatever I command" (Ezekiel 36:27, NLT).

I once thought life would be miserable if I became a Christian, but the truth is, I was miserable *not* being a Christian. Before I knew Jesus, my life was out of control. I was lost, scared, and confused. I lived a life of deception and lies, and I was emotionally and spiritually dead. But now, God has made me alive, and I am no longer confused about who I am because I am in Christ. I can't imagine my life without Jesus. Because He forgave me, I have been set free and am able to forgive those who hurt me. "It was for freedom that Christ set us free..." (Galatians 5:1, NASB).

Immediately after my salvation, God gave me a burden to pray for my family. During the next year, I watched as He radically transformed each one of my kids. That was fourteen years ago, and today, they are all in ministry and serving the Lord with all their hearts. "And we know that God causes everything to work together for the good of those who love God and are called according to His purpose for them" (Romans 8:28, NLT). And because of my love for my Lord and Savior, I am able to take the focus off my husband to meet all my needs and place my focus on Jesus and what He has done for me through His death on the cross. God has blessed me with a love for my husband above and beyond anything I thought possible, and we will be celebrating thirty-four years of marriage this year.

I am so grateful that God used the speaker's words that day to bring me to Him. What a release it was to acknowledge that the circumstances of my past had not made me what I was; they had simply revealed my sin that needed to be taken to the cross. Only then could I exchange my old life of shame, guilt, and fear for the loving, sacrificial life of Jesus. He made me a new creation, and turned my miseries into ministries. "Therefore, if anyone is in Christ, he is a new creation. The old has passed away; behold, the new has come" (2 Corinthians 5:17, ESV).

His grace has taken me from victim to victory. "The Lord is my strength and my song; He has become my victory" (Exodus 15:2, NLT).

Note from Lori

So there we were, all six of us, at the retreat. Kerry was on one end of the row and Donna was on the other. It was the last session on Sunday morning, and the speaker was giving her testimony. What none of us knew is that Donna had a secret she had hidden from everyone. She was afraid that if it was revealed, she would be rejected by our family, and she couldn't bear that. But when the Lord offered her forgiveness that morning, she knew that there was no other way to be set free. This is her story.

Believing a Lie: Donna's Story

Then we will no longer be like children, forever changing our minds about what we believe
because someone has told us something different
or because someone has cleverly lied to us and
made the lie sound like the truth...

Ephesians 4:14 (NLT)

When I was a freshman in high school, I began dating a guy who was two years older than me. Once we began dating, I had no interest in dating anyone else. Being young and thinking I was in love, I convinced myself that I had found Mr. Right. Fred became everything to me, so much so that even after he graduated and enlisted in the Marines, I continued to wait for him. By the time I graduated two years later, he was stationed in Hawaii. I told my mom that

I wanted to marry him. How else would I be able to be with him?

To say that my mom was less than thrilled would have been an understatement. In fact, she tried everything in her power to change my mind. But I was determined and somehow convinced her that marrying him was in my best interest. My mom, my little sister, and I flew to Hawaii. While we were there, my mom told me she didn't want to leave me there with Fred. I knew she was struggling with my decision to marry him, but I had made up mind, and no one could have convinced me otherwise. We were soon married, and my new life with Fred began. However, things didn't go as I had planned. We didn't live happily ever after.

After only six months, I realized I had made a terrible mistake. Fred rarely came home, and when he did, we seldom spoke to each other. He had completely withdrawn from me and from our marriage, and I felt so alone. Among other things going on between us, I found out he had gotten into drugs, and I was scared. I knew what I needed to do, so I swallowed my pride and flew back home to Nebraska. Six months later, when he was finished with the Marines, he came home. We tried to make our marriage work again, but it didn't go well, and I didn't know where to go from there.

I got a call one day from someone wanting to talk to me about my cousin, Mick. Kerry and I had never met, but we ended up talking for hours. She told me she was moving to California with her little boy. Even though I was still married, I immediately asked if I could go with her. She was ecstatic to have someone go with her, so I sold all of my belongings, and we left within a month. Little did we know that we would someday become sisters-in-law.

A short time after she graduated from high school, Lori came to California to visit and ended up moving in with Kerry and me. When summer ended, their brother Dave came out to visit for a week, and we all hung out together. I got to know him pretty well, and I really enjoyed being around him. That week seemed to fly by, and I found myself not wanting him to leave. I was so confused about how I was feeling toward Dave because I was still married.

As the weeks and months went by, I continued to think about Dave and at the same time wondered if there was anything left of my marriage. I made it through the holidays, and I was looking forward to my first snow-free winter. One morning as I was getting ready for work, the doorbell rang. My mouth dropped open when I saw Fred standing there. I didn't know whether to be happy or sad. I really didn't think that there was anything left in my marriage, but I still didn't want to give up either. I decided I should give it one more chance. It wasn't long after we got back together that we realized it wasn't going to work, so I filed for a divorce.

Shortly after that, Dave moved to California and we began going out together. On our first date, we went to Magic Mountain. Other than the fact that I got sick on the rides, we had a great time. We continued to see each other almost every day, partying, playing cards, and just hanging out. I remember always thinking that he was such a nice guy, and I loved being with him. For the first time in a long time, I felt like my life was coming together. But that was all about to change.

I wasn't feeling well, so I decided to go to the doctor. I stood there in disbelief when he told me I was two months pregnant. *No wonder I got sick on the rides at Magic Mountain!* Knowing it was my husband's, I had no clue what I was going to do. The only thing I knew at that point was that I didn't want to get back with him. *How am I going to tell Dave? Will I lose him?*

I finally got up the courage to tell Dave I was pregnant. I was so relieved when he said it didn't matter to him, but I was still scared. Here I was, pregnant, getting a divorce, and starting a new relationship. Even though Dave said he would stand by me, I really didn't know where our relationship was headed. We continued to see each other for the next couple of months. Everything seemed to be going well until one day, out of nowhere, Dave told me that a friend had asked him to move up to Northern California. He decided to move, and I was shocked and devastated.

I don't know what I would have done without Kerry and Lori at that time. They were a huge part of my life. When it came time to have my baby, they were there for me every step of the way. I delivered a beautiful baby boy named Kiley. About a month after I got home from the hospital, I decided to move back home to Nebraska. My mom and I had always been close, but after being gone for over four years, I didn't know what it would be like living with my parents again. When I was growing up, there was a lot of tension in our home. I always remember my mom keeping dinner warm for my dad until he got off work. He would come home late almost every night, and most nights he had been drinking. He always provided for us financially, and I definitely didn't lack in the way of material things. But emotionally, I always seemed to be running on empty.

I had been home for about a month when Dave also moved back to Nebraska. We started seeing each other again, and the three of us moved into a house together. I thought everything was going to work out, but Dave continued drinking every day, smoking pot, and doing speed. It wasn't too long before I was drinking and doing drugs right along with him.

When Kiley was around two years old, I discovered I was pregnant again. When I told Dave, he told me that he didn't think we should have another baby right then. I didn't want to do it, but I was afraid I might lose Dave. I justified having an abortion by thinking that the baby probably would not be okay since I was doing drugs. However, in my heart, I knew it was wrong.

I set up the appointment, and Dave took me to the clinic. I was so scared and confused about what I was doing. When it was over, I went back into the waiting room, and he wasn't there. Every minute that passed seemed like an eternity. He finally came back and said he had been at the bar next door. I had never felt so abandoned and alone as I did that day, and I cried the entire two-hour drive home, feeling empty and ashamed.

No one ever talked to me about God while I was growing up, so I never even asked questions about who God was or if He even existed. And even though I didn't know who He was, I believed that someday He would punish me for what I had done. As the days, weeks, and months went by, I tried to block the abortion out of my mind and go on living my life as if it never happened. I didn't want anyone to know because I thought they would hate me. I continued to smoke pot and party, never telling anyone what I had done.

A year after my abortion, I started having terrible pains in my lower right side. I went to the doctor and was admitted into the hospital right away with a tubal pregnancy. They had to do surgery to remove my tube, which left me with only a fifty percent chance of getting pregnant again. I immediately thought this was the way that God was going to punish me, by not being able to have any more children. Dave was so scared that something would happen to me during surgery that he asked me to marry him at the hospital. I always teased him that he was scared into proposing to me! In February of 1979, we flew to Las Vegas to get married. I'm pretty sure I got pregnant on my wedding day, because Nikki, our little girl, was born almost nine months later. Looking back on that now, I realize that by God's grace, He gave me exactly what I thought I didn't deserve.

As our kids grew up, Dave and I fought a lot. He always provided for us financially, but even if he was home, he seemed to be somewhere else mentally. After work, he always went to the bar with his friends and usually didn't get home until around nine p.m. every night. This always left him very little time with me or the kids, but we always knew he loved us. I realized then that I had married someone just like my dad.

My kids were going to a private grade school, and I was glad that they were learning about God at an early age. I thought maybe this is what I was missing in my life, so I joined the church Dave grew up in for all the wrong reasons. We continued to party and live our lives the same as we always had.

In the summer of 1994, our lives were changed forever. Kiley was eighteen years old and Nikki was fourteen at the time. She was very athletic and played softball that summer. I started noticing that she always seemed to be tired. I took her to the doctor, and he said she shouldn't play softball for about two weeks because she had mono. After the two weeks were over, she went back to playing softball but still complained about being so tired.

She was getting ready to start her freshman year of high school but before she could play in any sports, she was required to take a physical. They did the usual blood tests, but I immediately had a sick feeling in my stomach when the doctor came back in and said he needed to take some more blood. After ten *very long* minutes, the doctor came in and said he wanted us to go to an oncologist right away. Right then, I looked at her and noticed that she was dressed in everything mismatched because it was homecoming spirit week at school. It broke my heart, because I had a feeling she wouldn't be going back for a very long time. We had no idea how sick she really was.

I called Dave and told him to meet us at the oncologist's office. We were then sent to the hospital for a bone marrow biopsy. After this was complete, we were sent home to wait for the results. We were only home for about half an hour and the phone rang. It was our doctor telling us she wanted us in her office right away. It was six p.m. Nikki was still drowsy from the biopsy, and she didn't want to get out of bed. She really didn't understand any of it at that point, but we had to get her up and go. All the way over there, I was hoping this was a horrible mistake.

We were sitting in the doctor's office waiting for the doctor to come in. When she did, we could tell by the look on her face that it was bad news. She said she was sorry to have to tell us that she was 99 percent positive that Nikki had leukemia. After she explained everything to us, she left for a few minutes. *This is it. The punishment for having my abortion has finally come. I took a child's life, so God is going to take my child away from me.*

The doctor came back in and told us she had made arrangements for us to go to the Mayo Clinic in Rochester, Minnesota. We had to be there early the next morning, which left us little time to get ready. We needed to call everyone and tell them what was going on. Since Nikki would be at the Mayo Clinic for about six weeks, her family and friends came out to tell her goodbye. We got very little sleep, if any, that night because we had to leave at four in the morning. The ride up there was so long. I think we were all in shock. Nikki looked in the window and imagined seeing herself bald and started to cry.

When we arrived, they began a long series of tests without delay. They started chemotherapy at once because they needed to get Nikki into remission as soon as possible because it would improve her chances. They reassured us that the cure rate was about seventy-five percent, which gave us hope, but seven days later, the leukemia cells were still present. Every week, they would do a spinal tap to see if she was in remission, but it wasn't until the third week of testing that we received the good news she was.

We had so many trials during this time. One of the most trying times was when Nikki had a major allergic reaction to the steroids they had to give her for treatment. The steroids put her into a deep psychotic depression, which caused her to try to take her own life. She spent three days in ICU at the local hospital and then was transferred by ambulance to the Mayo Clinic. They performed electric shock treatments to her brain, attempting to get her out of her coma-like state. After about one month, she was back to her normal self and we got to bring her home.

Even though I gave God the credit for saving Nikki's life, I was also angry at Him for what He put us through. I was trying really hard to hold everything together, but after two years of this roller coaster ride, I was ready to break. I hadn't slept through an entire night since Nikki's diagnosis, and my emotions were up and down all the time.

About this time, Lori called and said she was going to a retreat. If I agreed to go, the six of us would be going together. What I didn't know was that Barb, Shelly, and Ellen were all saved, so it was just Kerry and I that needed to hear the gospel. Dave and Nikki encouraged me to go. I didn't know how I felt about going, but I knew that I needed to do something.

The first night we were there, about fifteen women were sitting around in our room giving their testimonies. They were all excited about the things that God had done in their lives. I was thinking, *I don't belong here...these people are too far out there for me!* I remember going into the hallway, confused and angry, and wanting to go home. Barb came out and started talking to me. I asked her how they could all be in there praising a God who gave Nikki leukemia. I told her I wanted to go home and that I couldn't be like these women. But God had other plans for me, and I stayed.

The next day, Lori and I went to a class together. I couldn't even tell you what the speaker said because the whole time I kept thinking about how I had to tell her about my abortion. I truly believed all these years that everyone I knew would think I was a horrible person, and they would reject me if they knew what I had done. When I finally got up the nerve to tell her, she looked at me and said she loved me no matter what and that God could forgive *any* sin. I didn't think God could forgive me, but Lori told me I was believing a lie. Just hearing Lori say she loved me and that God could forgive me helped open up my heart to Him the next day. This was the first step in my eyes being opened to the truth.

It was Sunday morning, and the last speaker was giving her testimony. She shared with us the guilt she dealt with in having more than one abortion. I felt like she was talking directly to me. She told us that after she gave her life to Jesus and confessed her sins, she knew He had totally forgiven her. I couldn't figure out how He could forgive someone who had committed murder, but I really wanted God's forgiveness. At the end of the session, she gave us all a chance to repent and surrender our lives to Jesus. I immediately started to cry and raised my hand to accept Him as my Lord and Savior. A great feeling of peace came over me, and by His grace I was forgiven!

After the retreat was over, we went to spend the night at Vanessa's, a friend of Lori's, so we could share with each other what had happened at the retreat. I was so scared to tell everyone what I had done, but I knew that it was the next step in being set free of this burden I had carried around for so many years. When I told them, they started hugging me and telling me how much they loved me. What a huge relief! Proverbs 28:13 says, "He who conceals his sins does not prosper but whoever confesses and renounces them finds mercy."

It was finally time for us to go home. When I got there, Dave and Nikki could see just by looking at me that something was different. I was a new person with a new heart, and my life would never be the same. One of the things I faced once I came home and began living my new life was how to deal with the feelings of guilt I was still having over the abortion. I knew in my heart that I had been forgiven, but I kept having thoughts of what I had done. I wished I would have had the words from Psalm 103 at that time.

> He will not constantly accuse us, nor remain angry forever. He has not punished us for all our sins, nor does He deal with us as we deserve. For His unfailing love toward those who fear Him is as great as the height of the heavens above the earth. He has removed our rebellious acts as far away from us as the east is from the west. The Lord is like a father to His children, tender and compassionate to those who fear Him. For He understands how weak we are; He knows we are only dust.
>
> Psalm 103:9–14 (NLT)

It didn't happen overnight, but I began to realize that since God forgave me, I needed to move on. If God was not accusing me, I needed to stop accusing myself. I thought I had put everything behind me, but Dave and I continued to struggle in our marriage, no matter what we did.

I was getting ready to go on a trip and decided to leave my type-written testimony on the table for Dave to read. Before I left town, Kerry called and asked me to go to coffee. I never turn down a chance to have coffee with her, but by the sound of her voice, I knew she had something on her mind. She knew I was planning to leave my testimony for Dave because I had told her I wanted to let him know just *what* he had put me through.

When we sat down, she asked me if I was still angry at Dave for the abortion and also the fact that he left me there and went drinking. Before I could answer she asked me, "Have you forgiven him?"

Tears welled up immediately and I looked at her and asked, "When is this ever going to end?"

And she said, "When you forgive him."

We continued to talk things through, and I admitted that I hadn't even thought about my unforgiveness toward Dave. We talked about how forgiving him didn't mean that what he had done was right, but that I needed to forgive him because of what God had done for me. Colossians 3:13 says, "...Remember, the Lord forgave you, so you must forgive others."

Kerry prayed with me and asked God to help me fully surrender my sin of unforgiveness toward Dave. We prayed specifically that I would be able to forgive him before I gave him my testimony. I knew this was something I needed to do, but I didn't want to. I knew this would definitely be something only God could do through me.

Four days later, I was at my Thursday morning Bible study. We were watching a video, and the speaker was talking about women who "lock themselves in self-imposed prisons of guilt over having an abortion when God longs to forgive them." She said, "Women carry their guilt—and it not only affects them but their attitudes toward their world." She said we need to love and forgive others like God has done for us. It hit me like a ton of bricks. My heart was beating so fast I thought I was having a heart attack! Why couldn't I forgive Dave, especially since Jesus had forgiven me? I realized right then that if I continued to hold on to my anger and bitterness, my relationship with the Lord would be hindered, and I could not be the kind of wife that God had created me to be. When it came time for me to leave my testimony for Dave to read, I was able to give it to him and tell him that I had forgiven him. I prayed and asked God to help him receive it in love. God answered my prayer, and by His grace, our marriage was strengthened.

Kiley is now thirty-five years old, and God has blessed Dave and I with a grandson who is our pride and joy. Nikki is thirty years old and was married on September 10, 2004 to her husband, Jeff. When they decided to try to start a family, they didn't know if she would be able to conceive because of all the chemo and radiation. In 2006, they found out they were expecting their first child. We were so grateful to God for blessing them with this miracle. Our excitement was short-lived. We found out that their baby had Turner's syndrome and a severe heart defect. Six months into her pregnancy, they lost their little girl, Faith. Her name was inspired by the scripture Hebrews 11:1 (NIV): "Now faith is being sure of what we hope for and certain of what we do not see."

This was one of the hardest things for all of us to go through, but it was especially difficult for Nikki and Jeff. And even though Nikki grieved deeply for her little girl, she chose to trust God for His will in all of this. Everyone was able to see the supernatural strength that God gave her during this time. It was amazing. Many people kept asking her, "How can you be so strong, especially with your past and what you have been through?" Nikki told me that after watching me give in to the enemy of guilt and anger, she didn't want that for her life. She had learned from my mistakes, and she has been such an inspiration to me.

One of the things she said to me during this time was, "You cannot choose the life God gives you, but you can certainly choose how you live it." She has continued to show me that choosing to let God into your life is far better than trying to live in your own strength. We have watched as God has poured out His grace on their family. They now have two children: Averee, their two-year-old daughter, and Ryder, their little boy. The best news is that this October 2010, she will have reached her sixteenth year of being cancer-free!

This is a picture of Nikki and I

It has taken me awhile to understand all of the things that have taken place in my life, but I have learned over the years that God has everyone in a different place for His glory. It is only in God's timing that things can change.

I have been a Christian for fourteen years now, and God has blessed me in so many ways. It has taken me a lot of years to become the person I am today, and God continues to peel off the layers one by one. He says in Philippians 1:6, "And I am sure that God, who began the good work within you, will continue His work until it is finally finished on that day when Christ Jesus comes back again."

So with all that has happened in my life, God has been my guiding hand through it all and has never let me down. Whenever I start to feel those old feelings of anger and unforgiveness coming back, I will cling to Galatians 5:1, "It is for freedom that Christ has set us free, stand firm, then, do not let yourself be burdened again by binding you to sin."

Once in awhile, I still wake up with feelings of guilt about what I did, but then I think—TGIF— Thank God I'm forgiven! I am so excited about the years to come because I know Him now, and because of that I have eternal life.

Left to right: Donna, Kerry, Lori,
Ellen, Shelly, and Barb (in front)

Afterword:
Final Note from All of Us

We hope you read the introduction at the beginning of this book. If you didn't, please go back and read it now before you answer the following question:

So what about you? Are you a believer, an unbeliever, or a make-believer? Every one of us sisters thought we were okay. We were make-believers, in every sense of the word, and always tried to hide our secrets from each other. Some of us thought our religion would get us into the kingdom of heaven. Most of us, as you have read, thought being good enough should count for something while some of us didn't have a clue and didn't even think about God at all. But none of us ever thought we were in danger of going to hell. We were deceived. Matthew 7:21–23 (NLT) says:

Not all people who sound religious are really godly. They may refer to Me as "Lord," but they still won't enter the Kingdom of Heaven. The decisive issue is whether they obey My Father in heaven. On judgment day many will tell Me, "Lord, Lord, we prophesied in Your name and cast out demons in Your name and performed many miracles in Your name." But I will reply, "I never knew you. Go away; the things you did were unauthorized."

It wasn't until God came in and caused us to be born again and turned our lives right-side up, that we saw Him for who He really was and began to live lives that were real and genuine and lasting.

For you have been born again. Your new life did not come from your earthly parents because the life they gave you will end in death. But this new life will last forever because it comes from the eternal, living word of God.

1 Peter 1:23 (NLT)

This new life that we have been talking about is not from man but from the Spirit of God. "It is the Spirit who gives eternal life. Human effort accomplishes nothing..." (John 6:63, NLT).

If you know that you want a new life, a life that comes from the Spirit of God, but you don't know how to go about surrendering your life to Him, breathe an earnest prayer to God something like this:

> Dear God, I know You will not reject a broken and repentant heart. I need to be saved and know I cannot save myself. I confess my sins, and I want to surrender my life to You right now. Please forgive me for thinking I could ever be good enough on my own. Thank You for sending Your one and only Son, Jesus, to take the punishment for me by dying in my place so that I can have new life and live with You forever. In Jesus's name, amen.

We hope and pray that your life has been touched by God's amazing grace and love. We will continue to pray for you, our family and friends and won't stop until they all fall down...to worship!

Thank you for taking time to read our story. If you would like to contact us for a conference or to let us know how God touched you through this book, you can e-mail us at our website, www.theyallfalldown.org. We would love to hear from you!

e|LIVE

---

listen|imagine|view|experience

AUDIO BOOK DOWNLOAD INCLUDED WITH THIS BOOK!

In your hands you hold a complete digital entertainment package. In addition to the paper version, you receive a free download of the audio version of this book. Simply use the code listed below when visiting our website. Once downloaded to your computer, you can listen to the book through your computer's speakers, burn it to an audio CD or save the file to your portable music device (such as Apple's popular iPod) and listen on the go!

How to get your free audio book digital download:

1. Visit www.tatepublishing.com and click on the e|LIVE logo on the home page.
2. Enter the following coupon code:
   afe8-16e7-a0b7-bb2e-0666-0d25-1592-f204
3. Download the audio book from your e|LIVE digital locker and begin enjoying your new digital entertainment package today!